Pathway to Promotion

Alan Leonhardt

Pathway to Promotion

Copyright © 2020 by Alan F. Leonhardt

All Rights Reserved. No part of this publication may be reproduced, stored in a retrieval system, or transmitted in any form or by any means - for example, electronic, photocopy, and recording - without the prior written permission of the publisher. The only exception is brief quotations in printed reviews.

Published by Lionheart Publications, a division of
Lionheart Ministries
1600 W. State Rd
Hastings, MI 49058
alanleonhardt@gmail.com

Unless otherwise indicated, scripture is taken from the New King James Version. Copyright © 1982 Thomas Nelson, Inc. Used by permission. All rights reserved.

Scripture marked NIV is taken from the Holy Bible, New International Version Copyright © 1973, 1978, 1984 by International Bible Society. Used by permission of Zondervan. All rights reserved.

Scripture marked AMP is taken from the Amplified Bible. Copyright © 1954, 1958, 1962, 1964, 1965, 1987 by the Lockman Foundation. Used by permission.

Cover design by Kathy Mayo

ISBN 978-1-7348354-0-3

First edition

Printed in the United States of America

Other Book by Alan Leonhardt

Spirit World, 2019

In Pastor Alan's book "Spirit World," he speaks from experience about moving successfully in the Holy Spirit. This is a rare teaching. I highly recommend it.
~ Troy Townsend, Gilead Healing Team, Lansing, MI

First, let me say, I love Spirit World. I just received it and read the first chapter. Wow! Every theological doctrine, including eschatology (the study of end times), in just twenty pages! Amazing and brilliant. I didn't want to stop reading and can't wait now for chapter two and beyond.
~ Dave Williams, Dave Williams Ministries, Lansing, MI

Rev. Leonhardt's book, "Spirit World," is an essential book for your collection on the Holy Spirit. It is well written, insightful, and full of personal stories that make the content come to life. I appreciate that it is Scriptural and practical. It also comes from a life of experience in walking with the Holy Spirit. Pick up a copy for yourself and a friend, today!
~ Chris Palmer, Light of Today Ministries, Farmington Hill, MI

Dedication

I want to dedicate my all books to my wife Nicole, my four beautiful daughters, and the next generation.

> *One generation shall praise Your works to another,*
> *And shall declare Your mighty acts.*
> *— Psalm 145:4*

We have an obligation to pass on our wisdom and experience to the next generation. My biggest inspirations are my children. I want my ceiling in life to be their starting place and platform.

If we are wise, we will admit that we all stand on the shoulders of great men and women who have mentored us with the sacrifice of their lives. If someone can glean any good thing from my books that will help establish them and give them greater endurance to finish their race, then I will have done my job.

Contents

Introduction 7

Chapter 1
    Through Fire and Through Water 13

Chapter 2
    The Lion and The Bear 27

Chapter 3
    Honor and Submission 45

Chapter 4
    The Wilderness and The Promised Land 65

Chapter 5
    Approved or Disqualified 81

Chapter 6
    The Mindset of a Winner 101

Chapter 7
    The Storms of Life 117

Chapter 8
    Loving the Praise of Men 137

Chapter 9
    Guarding Against Sexual Lust 161

Chapter 10
    Good Parenting Brings Promotion 191

Chapter 11
    Look to the Reward 211

*We must adopt a philosophy
of life-long learning*

Introduction

PROMOTION COMES FROM GOD

For exaltation (promotion) comes neither from the east nor from the west nor from the south. But God is the Judge: He puts down one, and exalts another.
— Psalms 75:6-7

I was working for a fast-food restaurant and the night shift manager's position became open. I just knew I could handle it and that the position was for me. When I approached the General Manager and verbalized my ambition, she responded with a stoic facial look (otherwise known as "the poker face"). I advised her to not waste time seeking an unknown for the job because I could do it. Well... she didn't take my advice and hired someone else, who ended up stealing from the restaurant.

Another fast-food restaurant just down the street from where I worked advertised for an assistant manager's position. I quickly turned in my resume and was hired. The salary was even better than the night manager's salary, you know, that position that should have been mine but I was overlooked by the manager who mastered the art of facial stoicism (i.e. the poker face).

The moral of the story is that when it's your time for promotion, God will find a way of getting it to you. He is not limited by your present employer or situation. He can open doors that no man can shut and shuts doors that no man can open (see Revelation 3:7).

> Bondservants, obey in all things your masters according to the flesh, not with eyeservice, as men-pleasers, but in sincerity of heart, fearing God. **And whatever you do, do it heartily, as to the Lord and not to men,** knowing that from the Lord you will receive the reward of the inheritance; for you serve the Lord Christ. But he who does wrong will be repaid for what he has done, and there is no partiality.
> — Colossians 3:22-25

Whatever you do, do it heartily to the Lord. It's God who ultimately promotes. He may use man to do it but it comes from Him. You work for God, and since He's the one to promote you, you should seek to be a God-pleaser and not just a people-pleaser. God sees your work done in secret and will reward you openly. As a Christian, you should strive to do things with excellence because you serve a God of excellence.

GOD'S TESTING WILL REFINE YOU FOR GREATER PURPOSES

> But He knows the way that I take; When He has tested me, I shall come forth as gold.
> — Job 23:10

God refines and tests us in many ways. He tests our faithfulness, diligence, perseverance, and obedience. He tests us and refines us so that He can bring us into our God-given purpose. There are many character flaws in each one of us that we cannot change through our own strength or will alone; we need the refining process of the Holy Spirit. Even Jesus went through forty days of testing in the wilderness. The good news is that when He graduated from His testing, He walked in the great power of the Holy Spirit.

> *Now when the devil had ended every temptation, he departed from Him until an opportune time.* ***Then Jesus returned in the power of the Spirit to Galilee,*** *and news of Him went out through all the surrounding region.*
> *— Luke 4:13-14*

YOUR INNER KINGDOM WILL DETERMINE YOUR OUTER KINGDOM

> *"Therefore give to Your servant an understanding heart to judge Your people, that I may discern between good and evil. For who is able to judge this great people of Yours?"*
> *— I Kings 3:9*

> *And God gave Solomon wisdom and exceedingly great understanding, and largeness of heart like the sand on the seashore.*
> *— I Kings 4:29*

What came first, the expansion and wealth of Israel, or the wisdom and expansion of King Solomon's heart? It was after God brought expansion to Solomon's inner kingdom that the outer kingdom prospered. Solomon and the kingdom of Israel became a wealth magnet.

We must adopt a philosophy of life-long learning. Read books, take classes, learn a skill, watch YouTube videos, go to seminars, and most of all, renew your mind with the Word of God. There is no counsel or understanding against God's Word.

Find a "Read the Bible Through a Year" reading program. Read a chapter of Proverbs a day.

I absolutely love this quote from Jim Rohn, a multi-millionaire motivational speaker: "*Learn to work harder on yourself than you do on your job. If you work hard on your job, you'll make a living, if you work hard on yourself you can make a fortune.*"

Stay teachable and pliable. Be willing to change your thinking when new truth is presented. Much of the truth we believe is only partial; there are deeper layers. I am NOT saying that truth changes. Truth is absolute. What I AM saying is that there is more truth to be revealed, and what we already know can be expanded. Don't be afraid of truth because it may demand something from you or convict you of sin. Accept that you must change and conform to new data. I have much more depth in knowledge today than I did ten years ago. There are many things I taught ten years ago from the pulpit of my church that I would consider shallow today.

> *Beloved, I pray that you may prosper in all things and be in health, **just as your soul prospers.** For I rejoiced greatly when brethren came and testified of the truth that is in you, just as you walk in the truth. **I have no greater joy than to hear that my children walk in truth.***
> *— III John 1:2-4*

Here we have the same concept in the New Testament as in the life of Solomon in the Old testament. Our inner kingdom (our soul realm) must expand before our outer kingdom expands. Our health and prosperity in all things are contingent upon our soul prospering. And how does our soul prosper? By knowing and walking in truth. As we receive more light, we must walk in that light.

Introduction

> *But the path of the just is like the shining sun, that shines ever brighter unto the perfect day. The way of the wicked is like darkness; They do not know what makes them stumble.*
> — Proverbs 4:18-19

May your heart be open and teachable to the truths in this book. Some subjects may be difficult because you and I don't want to admit failure. Receive the divine warning and correction. Get up and try again. God wants to build you up, not beat you up. He is a good father and wants all His children to be successful and find the path to promotion.

Pastor Alan Leonhardt D.Th.

Although we must go through a cleansing and refining process, we have a promise that we will not be harmed

Chapter 1

Through Fire and Through Water

*For You, O God, have tested us;
You have refined us as silver is refined.
You brought us into the net;
You laid affliction on our backs.
You have caused men to ride over our heads;*
**we went through fire and through water;
but You brought us out to rich fulfillment.**
— Psalm 66:10-12

Before the periodic table, primal man understood the universe to have only four basic elements: Earth (solid mass), Wind (air, gas), Water (liquid) and Fire (plasma, combustion). Each of these elements was essential for survival. Mankind's interdependence to the natural world must have seemed very mystical. Personally, I don't think we should ever lose that awe of God and His creation, no matter how sophisticated we become.

Water: Just as we need fire and water to survive in the natural, so also, we need the fire and water of the Holy Spirit to survive spiritually. Two-thirds of the Earth's surface is covered by water; amazingly enough, two-thirds of the human body is comprised of water. After three or four days without water, your internal organs begin to shut down. Water is essential for life and a great symbol for the life-giving Holy Spirit.

> *For I will pour water on him who is thirsty, and floods on the dry ground; I will pour My Spirit on your descendants, and My blessing on your offspring.*
> *— Isaiah 44:3*

Fire: Without fire, there would be no heat, cooking or metallurgy. Fire illuminates, purifies and can be harnessed for energy. Fire is also a great symbol for the Holy Spirit (see Matthew 3:11-12). We need the fire of the Spirit in our lives. The Holy Spirit uses the purifying agents of fire and water to form our character. His objective is not our destruction, but to bring us out to rich fulfillment.

One truth that I heard little about as a new believer in Christ was that **God will test you before He promotes you**. I didn't hear many teachings on the testing of God, or that He would use adversity to mold character in my life. I was taught about the abundant life that awaited my decision to be a follower of Jesus (see John 10:10, so true). The truth that God was about to rock my world and begin a refining process was not on the brochure. To be brutally honest with you, I haven't exactly been forthright on that point when giving altar calls either. I will say things like, "Come as you are. God cleans His fish after He catches them." It just doesn't seem right telling folks, "Come to Christ and He will heat the kiln, throw you in the molten lava and hey, let's see what nasty things come to the surface that need to be skimmed off."

The beautiful truth is, God wants to bless us. He is saving us from ourselves. Before He can bring us into certain blessings and promotions He must make sure we are ready and prepared to handle them. He's not some sadistic cosmic party crasher delighting in messing with your life. He is good, and every good and perfect gift comes from Him (see James 1:17). Any testing or hardship that He allows will do us good in the end. After going through the fire and the water He brings us out to rich fulfillment. **God loves us enough to complete what He started.** He will not abandon us half-way in life's journey. No matter what comes, we can be confident in His loving motive.

> *Being confident of this very thing, that He who has begun a good work in you will complete it until the day of Jesus Christ.*
> *— Philippians 1:6*

> *But He knows the way that I take;*
> *When He has tested me, I shall come forth as gold.*
> *— Job 23:10*

I have heard it said that **your gifting will take you where your character can't keep you**. In other words, your gifting will promote you and make room for you, but if you have a bad character you will crash and burn. You will not be able to sustain yourself in any exaltation. You will be a shooting star; a rapid riser that burns out fast. We need God to develop good character in us so we can handle and sustain His abundant life.

You will see this pattern over and over in the Bible. Before honor is humility. Before God can bring you out to rich fulfillment, you must go through fire and through water. The elements of fire and water are tools for cleansing and refinement, not destruction.

> *When you pass through the waters, I will be with you;*
> *And through the rivers, they shall not overflow you.*
> *When you walk through the fire, you shall not be burned,*
> *Nor shall the flame scorch you.*
> — Isaiah 43:2

Although we must go through a cleansing and refining process, we have a promise that we will not be harmed. In the book of Daniel, three young men served in the court of King Nebuchadnezzar. While serving there, the king erected a giant golden statue (probably of himself, I'm pretty sure most despots are narcissistic) and wanted everyone to worship it when the symphonic orchestra began playing (see Daniel 3:1-6). Well because these three Hebrew men would not worship an idol, old king Nebuchadnezzar had them bound and thrown into a fiery furnace.

> *Then Shadrach, Meshach, and Abed-Nego came from the midst of the fire. And the satraps, administrators, governors, and the king's counselors gathered together, and they saw these men on whose bodies the fire had no power; the hair of their head was not singed nor were their garments affected, and the smell of fire was not on them.*
> — Daniel 3:26b-27

When these men were thrown into the fire, they were bound (see Daniel 3:23), **but the fire burned only the ropes that bound them**. The king saw them standing loose, and a fourth man like unto the Son of God walking in the fire with them (see Daniel 3:25). You will go through the fire also but you will not be burned. **Only the ropes that bind you will be incinerated!** God will always keep His promise and not allow the fire to scorch you. Jesus was revealed in the fire, and He will reveal Himself to you in greater dimensions and show you His glory.

Even the unbelieving world will see that God is with you. The fire is designed to burn off the ropes that bind you and bring you into greater freedom.

When the children of Israel went through the Red Sea, their Egyptian captors tried to follow them through that baptism and were drowned (see Exodus 14:22 & 28). When you go through the water of purification you will not be drowned, but those things that want to keep you enslaved will be destroyed in the water. All must pass through the fire and the water. Before your promotion you must humble yourself under the mighty hand of God that He may exalt you in due time (see 1 Peter 5:8). You must trust Him and follow Him through the floods. Your destiny and more of the resurrection life of Jesus is waiting for you on the next shore.

God is not trying to hurt us; He's trying to help us. As we pass through the fire and the water, those things that bind and enslave us are destroyed. The truth is, there are things about our character that we cannot change by the strength of our will alone. God has to use outward forces to bring the best out of us. Though we have to go through fire and through water, He is bringing us out to abundance and rich fulfillment.

> *For You, O God, have tested us;*
> *You have refined us as silver is refined.*
> *You brought us into the net;*
> *You laid affliction on our backs.*
> *You have caused men to ride over our heads;*
> ***we went through fire and through water;***
> ***but You brought us out to rich fulfillment.***
> *— Psalm 66:10-12*

TRAINED BY THE TESTING

Now no chastening seems to be joyful for the present, but painful; nevertheless, afterward it yields the peaceable fruit of righteousness to those who have been trained by it.
— Hebrews 12:11

The testing of fire and water will only yield the peaceable fruit of righteousness if we are trained by it. God's chastening process will not work on some people who refuse to change and receive the correction.

You and I both know some people (who will go un-named) who have gone through mammoth divine discipline and came through it, clueless... You think to yourself, "How much lower can this person go?" Luke 15: 11-24 tells of a young rebellious man working for a local pig farmer and getting buzzed from breathing the toxic methane manure. He's so starved that he's sneaking bowls of pig slop to stave off hunger pangs. The only thing left is for the earth to open up and swallow him alive. All the while, a loving Father waits for his son to return; waiting for him to get a clue. Would he just humble himself and come home?!? No sooner does the son come home when the Father runs to him with an embrace. He throws a princely robe on his son and puts a gold ring on his finger. We may get frustrated over the stubborn resistance of some folks to change, but never doubt the fortitude and patience of a loving heavenly Father.

It's important that we don't ignore the beckoning of God. We need to be trained by correction and personally own what God is saying to us. I always get an inward snicker when I preach a very convicting point in my sermon and a husband or wife will elbow their spouse. Or, they approach me after church and tell me, "Oh man, if only so and so was here. He really needed to hear that." Before we look at the faults of others, we should always look at ourselves first.

> *For if we would judge ourselves, we would not be judged.*
> *But when we are judged, we are chastened by the Lord,*
> *that we may not be condemned with the world.*
> *— 1 Corinthians 11:31-32*

The most important judgment that you and I will go through is not something far off in the future after death, it's **the believer's self-judgment**. If we would judge ourselves, we will not be judged and chastened by the Lord. We must keep a tender conscience. We must be willing to change. Have you ever spoken words like, "This is who I am and everyone had better just deal with it"? God does not want to destroy your individuality; He celebrates your uniqueness. You must admit though, there are things about your personality, disposition, and character that need a little tempering. The Bible says that we are being changed from glory to glory and from faith to faith (see Romans 1:17, 2 Corinthians 3:18). You and I are being changed and conformed to the image of God's Son, Jesus (see Romans 8:29). If you're not changing then you risk running head-long into God's chastening. Change is good. God is changing you and me into something beautiful and astounding.

> *For we are His workmanship, created in Christ Jesus*
> *for good works, which God prepared beforehand*
> *that we should walk in them.*
> *— Ephesians 2:10*

"For we are His workmanship." The word "workmanship" is the Greek word "poiema", from which we get the English words, "poem" and "poetry". God is a master artisan and He is creating a beautiful expression of His glory out of our lives. "We are a soliloquy of word pictures and images that inspire the highest ideals from the people in our life." No, God is not trying to destroy us; He is trying to create something so strikingly stunning out of our lives that people will have no choice but to admit that this is a work of God.

Be willing to change; it's important. The Word of God states, *"Because they do not change, therefore they do not fear God"* (Psalm 55:19b). So, not being willing to change is a total lack of reverence for God almighty.

Be willing to receive correction. The Word also states that an unwillingness to receive correction is a sign of stupidity. *"Whoever loves instruction loves knowledge, but he who hates correction is stupid"* (Proverbs 12:1).

If one refuses to change and be trained, he risks becoming obsolete, archaic, a prehistoric relic, an unusable castaway. Unwillingness to be changed and transformed will cause you to become extinct. There have been several mass extinction events in history; events like the ice age, a universal flood (Noah's flood) and meteor strikes. Flora and fauna that could not adapt to a changing environment have become extinct. You can still visit their fossilized bones and leaves at a museum of natural history. The world moves on; move with God or become a fossil.

"Oh man, that's harsh preacher."

No, what's really harsh is watching good folks not fulfill their God-given destiny because they are fearful and stubborn. Unfortunately, pastors and teachers cannot take your tests for you. We can only watch, pray and teach the Bible. We must all work out our own salvation with fear and trembling (see Philippians 2:12-13).

Preachers are being changed and transformed as well. Many times, you will be able to see their issues and blind spots. You will probably watch in glorious Technicolor as they are tested by fire. It's to YOUR advantage and blessing that the preacher makes it through his/her testing. His/her promotion is the promotion of the local church. Instead of broadcasting to everyone how spiritual you are by identifying the preacher's blind spot, you should rather pray for spiritual leadership. That would be a true mark of spirituality. If you want to reap mercy you must sow mercy. There will be a time when your blind spot will be revealed to all the world. At that time, you won't need ridicule and judgments, you'll need the prayers of the saints.

THROUGH THE FIRE AND WATER OF THE HOLY SPIRIT

Then Eleazar the priest said to the men of war who had gone to the battle, "This is the ordinance of the law which the LORD commanded Moses: "Only the gold, the silver, the bronze, the iron, the tin, and the lead, everything that can endure fire, you shall put through the fire, and it shall be clean; and it shall be purified with the water of purification. But all that cannot endure fire you shall put through water. And you shall wash your clothes on the seventh day and be clean, and afterward you may come into the camp."
— Numbers 31:21-24

Fire and water are emblems or symbols of the Holy Spirit in the Bible. Notice in the above verses that everything had to be purified by fire or water before it was accepted in the camp. Our God is a consuming fire and all must be purified and sanctified when they come to Him. Fire and water cleanse in different ways; the fire is used to cleanse metals and precious stones, and water is used to purify clothes. It is interesting to note that metals, precious stones, and white garments are all symbols of the righteousness of the saints. Our works will be put through fire, and we are clothed with the righteousness of Christ. We must make sure that we purify our hearts with obedience and that we maintain right motives (see 1 Peter 1:22). Every believer is responsible to judge his/her own heart and to wash his/her robes and make them white in the blood of the lamb (see Revelation 7:14). There is coming a day when all of our works will be tested by fire.

> *For no other foundation can anyone lay than that which is laid, which is Jesus Christ. Now if anyone builds on this foundation with gold, silver, precious stones, wood, hay, straw, each one's work will become clear; for the Day will declare it, because it will be revealed by fire; and the fire will test each one's work, of what sort it is. If anyone's work which he has built on it endures, he will receive a reward. If anyone's work is burned, he will suffer loss; but he himself will be saved, yet so as through fire.*
> *— 1 Corinthians 3:11-15*

Notice that this fiery test does not destroy you; it just burns off the stubble and dross. The thoughts of the heart and inner motivations are everything with God. *"For as a man thinks in his heart, so is he"* (Proverbs 23:7). Even if your motive is gold, it will still be refined. Your golden heart may only be 95% pure.

When I was a youth pastor, a young man made a decision for Christ for the purpose of being close to a girl in the youth group (it happens, raging hormones). When the girl rejected him, fire swept over his soul and his motivations for serving Jesus were coming under a test. What was his foundation? Was it Jesus, or a relationship with a girl? He passed his test and chose to stay with the Lord. There is no other foundation to build upon than a love for Jesus Christ. If your commitment to Christ has ulterior motives, those motives will be put to the test. The Holy Spirit is working in our lives to bring us to a place where we can handle more. He is working for your promotion! Let's look at the emblems of the Holy Spirit and see what it can teach us about the person and work of the Holy Spirit in the life of a believer.

The emblems of the Holy Spirit teach us much about the person and work of the Spirit. One emblem in itself is not enough to give us a complete picture. Our God is too big to be contained in any one box. We cannot choose just one favorite emblem that makes us feel good and minimize all others. If there was a favorite among Christians, it would be the symbol of the dove. Who doesn't love the dove? It is gentle, it symbolizes peace, and it coos to you and comes from heaven. But this is not all there is; there are many other facets of the Holy Spirit to consider.

Here are some of the emblems:

- **Dove** (see Matthew 3:16) – Peaceful, gentle, comes from heaven. The Holy Spirit brings us supernatural peace to overcome the stress and challenges of life (see II Thessalonians 3:16, Isaiah 26:3).
- **Wind** (see John 3:8, Acts 2:2) – The Holy Spirit is invisible but His effects can be seen and felt. Wind is sovereign. You don't dictate which way the wind should blow. Wind can refresh but also can be a destructive hurricane or tornado. As a believer, you can discern the direction of the wind and what the Spirit is doing.

- **Water** (see Acts 2:17, Isaiah 44:2) – Water is life-giving. Without it, there could be no life on this planet. The Spirit gives life to all. Water is reflective and we can see what sort of person we are. Water cleanses and purifies.
- **Oil** (see Psalm 133, James. 5:14) – Oil is symbolic of the Spirit's healing power. In the Old Testament, individuals were anointed with oil when set in the office of Priest, King or Prophet. In the New Testament, all believers are anointed by the Holy Spirit (see 1 John 2:20). The oil symbolizes the enablement of the Holy Spirit who empowers us to do the work of the ministry.
- **Fire** (see Matthew 3:11, Acts 2:2-4) – Fire energizes. Fire illuminates (brings spiritual revelation), and fire purifies.

In Exodus 3:1-5, Moses is on the backside of the desert living out his life in simplicity and obscurity. He spots a strange thing on the side of a mountain; a bushy tree is burning but is not consumed. What kind of extraordinary fire is this that burns but does not consume? As Moses approaches the flame the voice of God speaks and tells him to remove his sandals because he is on holy ground.

Every believer in Christ should be like this burning bush. We should be ablaze with the Spirit. The Spirit burns but He does not consume and destroy us. What is the bush without the flame? It is just a mundane thing. But when it is ignited with the flame of God it becomes a sign to the world. The burning bush becomes a holy vessel for the Almighty to speak through.

Do not despise the fire. You are not meant for the mundane. You are meant to be ablaze with the Spirit and set apart for His glory.

As the children of Israel were trudging through the wilderness, they were led by a pillar of smoke and fire (see Exodus 40:34-38). In the New Testament book of Acts, 120 followers of Jesus were waiting in the Upper Room for the promised outpouring of the Holy Spirit. A mighty rushing wind came into the room and each person was filled with the Spirit and spoke in a language they had not learned. There appeared over their heads little fires (see Acts 2:2-4). Now each believer has a pillar of illuminating fire to lead us through the darkness of this world. The flame of the Holy Spirit and the Word of God are a lamp for our feet. Lead on, Holy Spirit, we will embrace your fire.

> *But the path of the just is like the shining sun,*
> *That shines ever brighter unto the perfect day.*
> *The way of the wicked is like darkness;*
> *They do not know what makes them stumble.*
> *— Proverbs 4:18-19*

The lion and the bear represent things that we overcome in obscurity before we earn the right to face and defeat our Goliath in the public arena.

Chapter 2

The Lion and The Bear

THE TEST OF FAITHFULNESS IN OBSCURITY

And Saul said to David, "You are not able to go against this Philistine to fight with him; for you are a youth, and he a man of war from his youth." But David said to Saul, "Your servant used to keep his father's sheep, and when a lion or a bear came and took a lamb out of the flock, I went out after it and struck it, and delivered the lamb from its mouth; and when it arose against me, I caught it by its beard, and struck and killed it. Your servant has killed both lion and bear; and this uncircumcised Philistine will be like one of them, seeing he has defied the armies of the living God." Moreover David said, "The LORD, who delivered me from the paw of the lion and from the paw of the bear, He will deliver me from the hand of this Philistine." And Saul said to David, "Go, and the LORD be with you!"
— 1 Samuel 17:33-37

Promotion in the Kingdom of God is different from the world's avenue of being upwardly mobile. In the Kingdom of God, we live mainly for an audience of one; God Almighty. In this world's system, we do our best to be noticed by anyone and everyone that matters. When we remember that all promotion comes from God, then our focus is readjusted and we remember who really matters. In this chapter, you will see that there is a faithfulness in obscurity that gets God's attention. God is the one who can get you noticed at the right time and in the right place, and by the right people.

As I consider the story of a boy confronting a lion and a bear to defend his sheep, I can't help but be in awe. To have the audacity and bravery to grab a lion by its beard, kill it with a sword, and rescue a lamb out of its jaws is the work of a seasoned warrior, not a shepherd boy. David was faithful before God in private long before he was esteemed by God publicly.

The lion and the bear represent things that we overcome in obscurity before we earn the right to face and defeat our Goliath in the public arena. If we cannot overcome our lion and bear, we will never be able to defeat our giant. When God anoints us with His Holy Spirit, He endows us to overcome and be faithful in the private arena as well as the public. The Spirit's power is not just for the pulpit, but for the private. His Spirit empowers us to be faithful, NOT just with the sacred (church stuff) but for the secular as well (holding a steady job).

In the lonely hills surrounding the small village of Bethlehem, David faithfully shepherded his father's sheep. When the prophet Samuel was sent to Jesse the Bethlehemite to anoint one of his sons as the future king of Israel, David, being the youngest of eight sons, was not even invited to the sacrifice and feast. Someone had to watch the sheep in the wilderness and it might as well be the runt of the litter (see 1 Samuel 16:1-13). When David was finally brought before the Prophet, the Lord spoke to Samuel and told him to pour the anointing oil on him, for he is the chosen one (see Exodus 30:22-33). The holy anointing oil found its way to a young teenager in an out-of-the-way place, and on unremarkable lonely hills. Isn't this the way of God; to bypass pedigree and outward appearance to call whom He chooses (see 1 Corinthians 1:26-31)?

When the enabling power of the Holy Spirit comes upon you, you are changed into a new person. With the Holy Spirit comes the spirit of faith (see 2 Corinthians 4:13). All things are now possible for him who believes (see Mark 9:23). When the kingly anointing comes upon you, there is an infusion of nobility, courage, and integrity. From among the ewe lambs arises a lion. From the youngest of eight sons arises a king. To think that this same Holy Spirit that empowered kings, priests and mighty prophets of the Old Testament also indwells New Testament believers (see John 14:15-18). God has truly made us Kings and Priests to the Most High God (see 1 Peter 2:9, Revelation 1:6 & 5:10).

Although the kingly oil may find us, there is no guarantee we will sit on the throne. Many are called but few are chosen. There is a journey we must take on the way to the throne. From the time we are called to the time we are separated to that call, **we must cross the bridge of faithfulness**. The lion and bear that *you* must overcome in obscurity may represent something different from *my* lion and bear. For instance, one person's lion and bear may be pride and lust, but for another, forgiving someone in their past and overcoming bitterness. Whatever your lion and bear are, some things always remain the same; everyone must be faithful in obscurity to be promoted publicly. "*Moreover it is required in stewards that* **one be found faithful**" *(1 Corinthians 4:2).*

FAITHFULNESS IN THE SMALL THINGS

> *His lord said to him, "Well done, good and faithful servant; you were faithful over a few things, I will make you ruler over many things. Enter into the joy of your lord."*
> — *Matthew 25:21*

Many people have problems starting small. Their vision and dreams are so huge that they don't know where to start. This can paralyze some to never move forward. Others are waiting for God to make something happen when God is waiting on them to take a baby step forward.

I've had some folks talk to me with frustration about their unfulfilled dreams. They were convinced that they had heard from God and because things didn't manifest, they doubt they can hear from God at all. After listening very sensibly to every detail of their story, I then ask, "In what way did you plan and prepare to make this vision happen?" After asking this, some folks just glare at me with glazed over, clueless eyes. Being somewhat mercy motivated, I don't want to lambaste folks with the brutal truth that it isn't God's fault, it's their OWN fault for not using their faith in small steps forward (short term faith goals). They DID hear from God, but because they did not understand the WAYS of God, it caused them a catastrophic failure. I don't want to leave you hopeless here. If you have made this error, then get back on the horse and seek God about your first steps. It may not be too late to fulfill what God originally put on your heart. Being faithful with the small steps forward will prepare you for your destiny.

Before David faced Goliath he went through a hardcore training time in the ruthless Judean hill country. He endured loneliness, frosty nights huddled close to a campfire. He experienced bruised feet and aching muscles from hiking after stray sheep and goats, not to mention the stress of being on constant alert for predators that could kill him and his flock.

As David submitted to God's training process, he was being conditioned for greater things. I can imagine him having a dream of one day being a heroic warrior in King Saul's army. Every day he would practice with his sling. Hour after hour in the heat and cold. After two or three years of practice, he knew the perfect weight of a stone that could be cast at deadly velocity. He found out that smooth stones from a creek bank are more aerodynamic and would have more proficient accuracy at greater distances. He discovered the range of his weapon and knew just the right distance to inflict on his target a precipitous death. With every rock hurled at a lifeless target, David was one step closer in realizing his dream; to follow his greatest hero, King Saul, into a glorious victory over the enemies of God and His people, Israel.

The sling was not going to be enough to earn a place in King Saul's army. David had to become proficient with the sword, staff, and bow. I can imagine him thrusting, blocking and striking at a tree stump. Shadow fighting with phantom enemies that would one day be a life-or-death struggle with a real opponent. As he leaped and jumped on the crags and rocky hills, his footwork became as graceful as a seasoned martial artist.

Then one day a stealthy lion crept into camp and latched onto a lamb. With the loud warning bleats of the flock, David's keen eye caught the image of a large cat prancing for cover to devour its catch. The unsuspecting ravenous pillager did not realize that the predator had now become the prey. David had been training for this day, honing his skills for such an opportunity. As the lion found what he thought was a secure spot to taste the lamb's warm blood, THUD! A smooth stone hit the lion's eye socket and sunk into his brain. Although the lion was not dead, it was so dazed and confused that in those crucial seconds of fight-or-flight, a powerful specter grabbed him by the beard. Then a polished sword, whetted to a razor's edge, came slicing into his throat. Game over.

What convinced King Saul to finally let the shepherd boy face Goliath in combat was that David had some battle experience. He had killed both the lion and the bear. Although David's victory over Goliath was miraculous, he came with a resume. There was probably no one in the camp who had single-handedly defeated two large carnivores. God was preparing David for future kingship one battle at a time. David's faithfulness to the small things in obscurity earned him the right to be victorious over a giant publicly.

You must not despise the days of small beginnings (see Zechariah 4:10). Everything is part of God's training program. You may not see how a seemingly dead-end job will facilitate your dream, but hindsight is 20/20. Every opportunity is useful and all things are working for you and not against you (see Romans 8:28). Many megalithic international corporations had their start in someone's basement or garage. You must be humble enough to submit to a mentor, training, education and the school of hard knocks. You must prove yourself faithful in the small things before you can rule over much.

I was going through a major discouragement as a young believer. After becoming *born again* when I was 20 years old, I joined a Christian rock band and we ministered at Jesus festivals and coffee houses for about two years. When the band broke up, I had to make a living so I was slinging hash at a Family Diner/Truck Stop. I didn't know what to do, and to make it worse, old friends would stop at the restaurant to see what had become of me. They would brag about their college degrees and lucrative new jobs.

One evening, I came home to my rented house that I shared with a couple of other guys, and as I went up the stairs to my bedroom God spoke to me in an audible voice, "*Feed my sheep.*" I wept and prayed for a while, not understanding what all this meant. This happened again two more evenings, "*Feed my sheep.*" The last time God spoke to me, He said, "*Feed my lambs.*" So for three evenings in a row, I heard God speak to me. The Bible says that in the mouth of two or three witnesses let every word be established (see 2 Corinthians 13:1). God spoke three times to fully confirm the calling He had on my life.

Folks would sometimes ask me what God's audible voice sounded like. All I can tell you is that it came from inside of me as well as outside of me. God's voice was the ultimate surround sound. With the very words spoken, there came an impartation to carry them out. I knew that God was calling me into a teaching/preaching/pastoral ministry. The third night that I heard God's audible voice, I was praying deeply in the Spirit and God spoke in an inner audible voice, "*I will begin to bring to you wisdom and knowledge. I will prepare you for the ministry I am calling you to. I will also show you a sign.*"

The next evening, I was reading my Bible and I read the story of the Magi who were led by signs in the heavens to worship the child, Jesus. A question arose in my mind, "I don't understand how God can condemn Astrology (looking to the stars for guidance), and yet lead these men to worship Jesus by the stars?" I no sooner formulated that question in my mind when one of my roommates came busting in the back door of our rented house, "Hey Al, the Lord told me to give you this book." The title of the book was "The Heavens Declare the Glory of God" by Marilyn Hickey (great book). On the first page of the first chapter was the answer to my question about the wise men. This was the sign! God was going to do what He said and prepare me for ministry. The short answer to my question is that God created the stars for signs and seasons (see Genesis 1:14), but man perverted them by worshiping them (see Deuteronomy 4:19). God sometimes speaks to us through nature and the cosmos (see Psalm 19 & Romans 1:20), but it is always confirmed by His Word. The Magi looked to the stars, found a revelation of the coming Messiah and worshiped the Christ child. The stars declare God's glory and will always lead to worshiping the Creator.

After God spoke to me audibly I made the mistake of telling some folks. It became quite evident why God had to speak to me audibly because men were not going to believe in my calling. The mocks and jeers were actually quite humorous, so let's just laugh at these lies: "Are you sure there isn't LSD tracers in your system still working themselves out?" "God doesn't speak to people audibly like that today." "Really, (enter the loud laughter here) I just don't see it. You just don't have the personality or the gifts to be in any kind of pastoral ministry." Apparently, some may think that you have to be a dry, stoic personality for God to use you in ministry. If you're too sanguine or have a sense of humor, you don't qualify. Fun people need not apply.

I'm telling you all this because I didn't go right out and print my cards. I didn't submit my pathetic resume to the first open church I was aware of. I submitted to schooling and training. I did every function in the local church you can think of: worship team/leading worship/home group leader/cleaning the church/greeter/usher/sound and media/youth ministry/children's ministry. I was faithful in giving my tithes and offerings, and in attending prayer meetings. I ministered in the nursing homes, the jails and all sorts of outreaches. After a few years my pastor allowed me to minister from the pulpit. It was not the Sunday morning service, it was the evening service. It wasn't until I was 41 years old that God separated me into my first Senior Pastor role. God's process may be a little different for you, and probably much faster (some of us have more bugs and kinks to work out of our system). But one thing is for sure, you must always be faithful with the little before God gives you more.

FAITHFUL IN WHAT IS ANOTHER MAN'S

*And if you have not been faithful in what is another man's,
who will give you what is your own?*
— Luke 16:12

Some would say, "I don't know what my vision is. Is there something wrong with me that I don't have a colossal ambition?" If you don't know what your vision is, then you need to partner with someone who does. As you support someone else's vision, God eventually will release vision to you. You may even get a vision within and under another man, or woman. (Some of God's best men are women.)

Let me give you an example; I have always had a vision to raise up the next generation in my church. I have always wanted to see a powerful Children's, Youth and Young Adults ministry. I want to see young people know God personally as opposed to just knowing about God. I want to see young people have life-changing encounters with God. The two sons of Eli; Hophni and Phinehas, were raised in the priesthood and taught all the knowledge of God. But the Bible says that they were corrupt and *did not know Him* (see 1 Samuel 2:12). Yet Samuel had an encounter with God as a child while attending to the Tabernacle late one night (see 1 Samuel 3). Samuel's encounter with God was so powerful that the voice of God was revealed to him and he became a mighty prophet to Israel.

The knowledge of God is in seed form until you experience God in a personal way. I have workers that are in complete agreement with this vision. They have adopted it and feel that it is their own. They feel called to serve under me and fulfill what God has called them to do, which is to work with children and youth; to raise up the next generation. As they put their hands to the plow, God has empowered them with personal vision under my larger vision.

This is not true of everyone. Some have huge apostolic vision and are called to lead networks of churches. Churches and Christian leaders feel led to come under their covering because they adopt the vision of the apostolic leader. They are in agreement with the style and philosophy of ministry held by an apostolic leader. This is another example of vision, under a broader vision.

The Lion and The Bear

If you think about it, ALL Christian leadership serves under a broader vision than their own. We all serve under the Kingdom of God and the commands and commissions of Christ. We all serve at His pleasure, for His glory, and for the expansion of His kingdom. We all serve something bigger than ourselves.

Before someone can be released into something greater they must prove themselves faithful in something smaller. They must be faithful in what is another man's. Before you are released into your own vision, you must prove yourself faithful in another man's vision. Before you can be a worship leader, you must serve under a worship leader. Before you can pastor your own church, you must serve faithfully under a pastor. Before you can own your own business, you must be faithful working for someone else. Before you can own your own home, you must be faithful with a rental. Etcetera, etc. etc... Unless you are faithful with another man's, who will give you that which is your own?

Before David became King, he was faithful serving under his father as a shepherd and he was faithful as a commander of a thousand men under King Saul.

> *Therefore Saul removed him from his presence,*
> *and made him his captain over a thousand; and he went*
> *out and came in before the people. And David behaved*
> *wisely in all his ways, and the LORD was with him.*
> *— 1 Samuel 18:13-14*

David didn't just leapfrog from killing Goliath to being king over all Israel. In the same way, when David was anointed by the prophet Samuel in the midst of his brothers, he didn't just walk into the throne room and assume his call. He went back to shepherding those few sheep in the wilderness. *We must be patient and let God move us step by step to our destiny.*

If you want people to faithfully serve under you, then you must sow seeds of faithful service into another's vision. You must sow the seeds of being a faithful follower to reap a harvest of those who will be faithful to you. Every seed yields fruit after its own kind.

FAITHFUL TO WAIT ON GOD FOR PROMOTION

Therefore humble yourselves under the mighty hand of God,
that He may exalt you in due time.
— 1 Peter 5:6

For those of us with ambition to do something great for God, staying humble and submitted to where we are can be as dramatically painful as a Greek Tragedy. Your pride will take you out of the will of God faster than the speed of light. I get it, you feel you are worth more and deserve more. That may be the case, but not at the expense of your peace of mind. You CAN elbow your way into a situation that you have not been prepared for and you will find a new definition for humility. It's called humiliation.

I always know when I am striving because I lose my peace. This is when I get alone with God and pray through to His peace (see Philippians 4:6-7). Trust me, you don't want to push ahead of God. If an army pushes forward too fast, they advance beyond the reach of their supply line. At this point they risk being outflanked and surrounded behind enemy lines. With supplies and ammunition depleted, they will eventually be overrun.

Your "due time" will be different than that of others. The worst thing you can do is to compare yourself with others. *"For we dare not class ourselves or compare ourselves with those who commend themselves. But they, measuring themselves by themselves, and comparing themselves among themselves, are not wise" (2 Corinthians 10:12).* You must become settled with who you are as a Christian man or woman. Your self-worth cannot be found in a position, achievement, title or net worth. If you are a pastor, your self-worth cannot be wrapped up in the size of your ministry. This is all easy to write about but harder to do. You and I know this stuff, but it's important that you get with God often and receive His affirmation. The laudations and admirations of man will never satisfy.

> The LORD is good to those who wait for Him,
> To the soul who seeks Him.
> It is good that one should hope and wait quietly
> For the salvation of the LORD.
> It is good for a man to bear
> The yoke in his youth.
> — Lamentations 3:25-27

When we wait patiently for God's appointed exaltation, it's not an idle wait. It is a hopeful wait as we work hard and display our faithfulness where we are. We wait with faith-filled expectations. We do our best to have a thankful attitude and make the best out of our situation. I have heard it said that "pain is inevitable, but misery is optional."

When this verse in Lamentations speaks of *"bearing the yoke in your youth,"* It's talking about paying your dues. It's about earning the right to lead. God has a specially designed process for every person. The bigger the calling, the deeper the process. God knows what needs to happen in you to prepare you for your destiny. You cannot out-flank the necessity of solid, life experience to enhance your anointing.

A guest minister came and spoke at our church. I love this guy. He has a way of challenging you to be better without making you feel condemned. As I was listening to him expound on the Word of God, the thought occurred to me, "Hey, I've preached on the same subject that he's teaching on; why does it seem so much richer coming from him?" The answer, is that experience and refined character causes an exponential increase of rich anointing on your life. Fresh oil from the presses of heaven is continually poured into, and out of, a yielded vessel. We hold this treasure in earthen vessels, and God has His favorite carafes to pour out the elixir of life. Some are vessels of honor, chosen for the Master's use because they have borne the yoke of life experience.

Exaltation comes from God, He puts down one and raises up another (see Psalm 75:6). He can remove people from positions as well as promote them. John the Baptist said, "*A man can receive nothing unless it has been given to him from heaven*" *(John 3:27)*. I will say this, you can grasp for something that has not been given to you from heaven and it will NOT turn out well. It's better to humble yourself under the mighty hand of God. He's a little smarter than we are, and He's been around a little longer. He knows you better than yourself. He knows what will ultimately fulfill you. He is preparing you for awesome things.

When we look at the word "wait" in the passage above (see Lamentations 3:25-26), the Old Testament Hebrew word is, qavah (kaw-vaw') Strong's #6960. This word means more than just waiting patiently. There is a picture of binding together, as in twisting. Imagine one strand of cable; now imagine two more strands twisted together with that one strand. That cable is more than three times stronger. The law of synergy takes effect and that cable is a hundred times stronger. A three braided cord is not easily broken (see Ecclesiastes 4:12). When we wait on the Lord we are twisting our lives around His strength. The strength of the Almighty is woven into our soul. This same word is also used in the well-known passage in Isaiah 40:31:

> *Have you not known? Have you not heard? The everlasting God, the LORD, the Creator of the ends of the earth, neither faints nor is weary. His understanding is unsearchable. He gives power to the weak, and to those who have no might He increases strength. Even the youths shall faint and be weary, and the young men shall utterly fall, but those who wait on the LORD shall renew their strength; they shall mount up with wings like eagles, they shall run and not be weary, they shall walk and not faint.*
> *— Isaiah 40:28-31*

As we wait on the Lord, strength is built in us that will sustain us for the long haul. Picture in your mind an old locomotive steam engine train. It takes time for the water to heat up and create steam pressure. As the engine steeps, the pressure builds to a point where it can be easily sustained over a long haul. Waiting on the Lord is not weakness, it is wisdom.

Consider how David waited on the Lord for the right open doors. He behaved himself wisely and faithfully along the way. Even when it was in his power to kill King Saul himself and assume the throne, he didn't. He waited on the Lord's timing and humbled himself under God's mighty hand. Don't be rash, and don't give up your peace of mind. Bind yourself together with the strength of the Almighty. He is the strength of your life (see Psalm 27:1 & 14).

> *I will instruct you and teach you in the way you should go;*
> *I will guide you with My eye.*
> *Do not be like the horse or like the mule,*
> *Which have no understanding,*
> *Which must be harnessed with bit and bridle,*
> *Else they will not come near you.*
> *— Psalm 32:8-9*

Notice in the above verses the Lord tells us not to be like the horse or the mule which takes a bit and bridle to control. You can't depend on them to respond to words alone, they must be forced or restrained to do the right thing. The horse has a tendency to run ahead and the mule has a tendency to stubbornly lag behind. You don't have to accept either scenario. You CAN be right on schedule with the Lord. When the children of Israel were on their journey through the wilderness, God led them with a pillar of cloud by day and a pillar of fire by night. If the cloud stayed in one place, they would stay, even if it was days or weeks. When the cloud advanced, they advanced. God is faithful. If you are seeking to know His will with all your heart, He will be faithful to speak to you and lead you.

I want to recap some of the areas of faithfulness that we have discussed before we move on. You must pass the test of faithfulness if you want to advance to maturity. Here are some bullet points:

- You must kill the lion and the bear in obscurity and then God will reward you openly.

The Lion and The Bear

- Be faithful in private devotions and Bible reading
- Be faithful in the small things and baby steps
- Be faithful in your financial investments into the Kingdom of God
- Be faithful to serve in another man's vision
- Be faithful to pray things through to peace
- Be faithful to wait on God's promotion

The principle of humility and submission coming before promotion and blessing is a theme woven into the tapestry of the Bible

Chapter 3

Honor and Submission

THE TEST OF AUTHORITY

Has the LORD as great delight in burnt offerings and sacrifices,
As in obeying the voice of the LORD?
Behold, to obey is better than sacrifice,
And to heed than the fat of rams.
For rebellion is as the sin of witchcraft,
And stubbornness is as iniquity and idolatry.
Because you have rejected the word of the LORD,
He also has rejected you from being king.
— 1 Samuel 15:22-23

The subject of authority and how we deal with authority is huge with God. There is no true promotion in the kingdom of God until you learn how to submit to authority. I would go even further to say that honor and submission to spiritual authority is THE issue in the whole Bible. Think about it, the first sin in the Bible has to do with honoring God and submitting to His authority. Because Adam did not pass his test of submission, he relinquished his right to rule; Adam was demoted. To think that you will not be tested in this area, and continue to be tested in this area, is to not understand the ways of God. If you are already in the Kung Fu defensive fighting position concerning this subject, even before you have heard me out, this may be an indication that we have some work to do.

The very word "submission" causes folks to bristle. The mind begins to immediately contort and justify fiercely its fleshly independence. The demonic hordes of hell are stirred up into an unreasonable rage at the very thought of submitting to legitimate spiritual authority. To be in rebellion is to operate in a demonic spirit of witchcraft. The verse above states that a rebellious person is unwittingly practicing witchcraft.

King Saul was rejected from being king because of stubbornness and rebellion. When you reject authority, you forfeit your right to have authority. You will see this downward pattern over and over in the Bible:

- **Pride**
- **Rebellion**
- **Deception**
- **Perversion**

You can see this clear downward pattern displayed in Romans 1:21-32. Almost always, when deception has run its course there is gross, twisted thinking and sexual perversion.

Saul's pride and rebellion led him to be so perverted and twisted in his thinking that he fell into depression, jealous rages, consorting with witches and killing innocent priests and their families (see 1 Samuel 21:6-19). Saul relinquished his right to rule and was rejected from being King of Israel. The following verse became the final epitaph of King Saul's life.

> *So Saul died for his unfaithfulness which he had committed against the LORD, because he did not keep the word of the LORD, and also because he consulted a medium for guidance.*

> *But he did not inquire of the LORD; therefore He killed him,*
> *and turned the kingdom over to David the son of Jesse.*
> — 1 Chronicles 10:13-14

If the downward spiraling pattern is true, then the upward path is equally true:

- **Humility**
- **Submission**
- **Revelation**
- **Promotion**

This upward pattern is best seen in Philippians 2:1-11. There is no better example of this pattern being displayed than by the Lord Jesus Christ. He humbled Himself and became a man; submitted to the shame of crucifixion; and then after His resurrection, was exalted to the right hand of God. To be promoted in God's kingdom, this is the only upward path for all spiritual leadership.

This principle of humility and submission coming before promotion and blessing is a theme woven into the tapestry of the Bible. *"Before destruction the heart of a man is haughty, and before honor is humility"* (Proverbs 18:12). Humility is a trait that yields to instruction. A humble person is teachable. A humble person can acquiesce to God's authority, while a prideful person disdains any form of reproof. Pride and rebellion go hand in hand. Where there's smoke there's fire, where there's rebellion there's pride and stubbornness.

> *If you are willing and obedient,*
> *You shall eat the good of the land.*
> — Isaiah 1:19

Is it possible for a person to be outwardly obedient while inwardly disdaining the very notion of conforming to instruction? The above verse states that we must be "willing" AND "obedient," then we will eat the good of the land. If conformity is only outward, eventually it will be discovered. An inward resentment can only be concealed for so long, and then it will rear its ugly head.

A family was sitting at the dinner table one evening. Their three-and-a-half-year-old toddler Johnny was in a highchair. The highchair was starting to be uncomfortable as the toddler was outgrowing it. Little Johnny decided he did not want to be restrained, so he wiggled his way to a standing position in the chair. Any good parent knows that standing in a highchair is a dangerous business.

So Dad scolds, "Sit down right now."

Little Johnny retorts, "NO!"

"Sit down right now or I'm going to whack you on the behind!"

"NO!"

At this, the Dad gets up, marches over to Johnny, gives him one whack on the butt and forces him down into the chair. Although little Johnny was compliant by force, he answered defiantly, "I'm standing on the inside!"

We must be WILLING and obedient to eat the good of the land. Have there been times when you were obedient to God but with great inner protest? Stubbornness is as iniquity and idolatry. Stubbornness doesn't have to make sense, because it's a spiritual thing. Independent spirits will stubbornly resist going along with the group. They will always insist on their own way. They are blind to any sacrifice for cohesion and unity. Some folks are so rebellious and independent that even when it's rational to conform and submit, they resist. Defying logic, they become an undertow, a drag on the team.

Our children need to be taught how to properly relate to authority. Their success in life is dependent on this. There is no way to get out of submission to authority. If your children will not submit to *your* authority as their parent, then outside authority will eventually restrain them. By "outside" authority, I am referring to the police and jail time. If you don't instill in your children a proper respect and honor for authority, then they will not respect God's authority. You must always uphold authority to your children; they must be taught to honor their parents, police officers and teachers. If you are always undercutting authority to your children, you are not doing them a favor. If you train your children to only submit to teachers they like, or only when they feel like it, you are following a recipe for disaster. If you are always making excuses for their bad behavior, you are protecting their rebellion and nurturing the rebellious nature. Of course, if you as the parent are rebellious, then you will impart that trait to your children. If you feel your child is being treated unfairly, then you need to go privately to the child's authority and try to work things out, but in front of your child, you must always uphold and honor authority.

AGREEMENT OR SUBMISSION?

If you were to ask anyone whether they are submitted to authority or not, without hesitation they will say "Yes." The reason most go along with their authority is because they agree with that authority. Submission by definition is yielding when you DO NOT agree. This is where your submission is really put to the test. How do you react when asked, or told, to do something you don't agree with?

Don't get me wrong, I am not advocating blindly following anyone. Nor am I talking about submitting to abusive authority. At the risk of oversimplifying: if your authority is not asking you to do something that violates the rightly divided Word of God, you ARE obligated to obey. On the other hand, if your authority or government is unjust, you are NOT obligated to obey. This is called "civil disobedience." Let me give you an example from the Bible.

In the book of Acts, chapter four, the ruling council in Jerusalem commanded the Apostles to not speak nor teach in the name of Jesus. The response of Peter and John was, *"Whether it is right in the sight of God to listen to you more than God, you judge. For we cannot but speak the things which we have seen and heard"* (Acts 4:19-20). Jesus commissioned His disciples to teach and preach in His name. The law of God is higher than the law of man. If your authority asks you to do anything that violates your conscience or the Word of God, you are NOT obligated to obey. Just don't use God for an excuse for your rebellion.

Once in a while a person will tell me that God told them to quit their job, divorce their spouse, or whatever. It's a dangerous game when you use the name of the Lord to justify your self-will. *"You shall not take the name of the LORD your God in vain, for the LORD will not hold him guiltless who takes His name in vain"* (Exodus 20:7). Using the name of the Lord in vain is more than cursing and cussing. If you say that God told you to do something, and He did not, you have just used the name of the Lord as an excuse for your rebellion. Did I mention that this is a dangerous game? God will never tell you to do something that offends the principles of scripture and His revealed character.

In a church setting, I find that folks can agree on central doctrine but disagree on style. Hands down, the majority of disagreement is on style. Should the pastor wear a tie or not? Should we sing all hymns or have contemporary music? Should the chairs be gray or 70's orange? Should we have Sunday school or a mid-week Christian Education night? You get the picture; there is a difference between style preference and the core doctrines of the church. The church around the world is very diverse. You CAN more easily find a church that you agree with on the central doctrine than you can in finding one that you agree with on style. At some point, you are just going to have to submit. You are not going to agree on everything in any community. Eventually, you must agree to disagree, agreeably. You and I have to learn to play nice with others in the sandbox. In any relationship you can't always have your own way; that's called selfishness. We must learn to play nice, make concessions for the sake of unity and share our toys. If you think that being a leader means you can always have your own way, you will end up leading only one person: YOURSELF.

What happens when your disagreements outnumber your agreements? You have multiple options: (A) You could stage a coup and overthrow the powers that be…?, (B) You could take a secret survey and find out who agrees with you and lead your followers someplace else…? or (C) You could leave secretly and then when asked about it say, "I am forbidden to talk about it" thus kicking open the doors of evil suspicions and conspiracy theories. I didn't specify that all these options are righteous, I'm just stating the options. This is where people fail their personal character tests the most. How you deal with disagreements and how you honor authority is huge in the Kingdom of God. There may be times when God would have you move out from under your present authority, but it needs to be done honorably if possible. *"If it is possible, as much as depends on you, live peaceably with all men" (Romans. 12:18).*

Disagreements aren't the only reason someone has to abandon an organization. There will be legitimate promotions that cause people to move on. Even in promotions there needs to be honor, respect and thankfulness toward the organization you're leaving. This will speak well of your character and you won't be burning your bridges behind you.

Let me toss a couple of terms out to you: **Passive Rebellion**, or **Loyal Opposition**?

Passive Rebellion: A person with this characteristic will pretend that they are submissive to the leadership but are inwardly always fermenting a disdain for authority. They slink around in the shadows and sow seeds of dissension every chance they get. Their hypocrisy matches that of Judas Iscariot; they will eat a covenant meal with you and then sneak off into the night to betray you to the highest bidder. Like Absalom, the son of King David, they appear to be the perfect example of what second-tier leadership should look like, BUT, secretly they gravitate to even the slightly disgruntled and dissatisfied and bring subtle doubts as to the trustworthiness and integrity of leadership. I have pulled many daggers out of the backs of fellow pastors who have been brutally betrayed by these sneaky, gutless cowards. Do you think that God will promote such behavior? Even if promotion comes to these people, they will reap a harvest of passive rebellious people who will do to them exactly what they have done to others. **And the harvest is always greater than the seed sown.**

Loyal Opposition: A person with this characteristic is just the opposite of a passive, rebellious person. If they disagree with leadership, they will not hide it. They will respectfully voice their opinion. And then if leadership does not take their advice, they will submit and support.

As a leader, I value the input and suggestions of those around me. Several brains are better than one. I think it's important to create an environment where suggestions are welcome. If you are insecure and defensive, you will squash any perceived challenge; any suggestion will be seen as a challenge or criticism to your authority. There is a difference between someone trying to overthrow authority and someone sincerely trying to help the goals progress. If you are always suppressing your loyal opposition, you may be stimulating passive rebellion in the ranks. We cannot be viewed as unapproachable by the Lieutenants we have surrounding us. There is amazing wisdom and insight that can be mined from the people around you. Most of the folks I know want to see things progress and move forward. People love being part of something successful. It's a big self-boost to have some ownership in decisions that advance and prosper the vision.

YOU MUST BE UNDER AUTHORITY TO HAVE AUTHORITY

Therefore submit to God. Resist the devil and
he will flee from you.
— James 4:7

There are many forms of spiritual warfare. One way to overcome demonic attack is to simply yield and submit to God. You cannot resist the devil if you are not submitted to God. If you try, you will be the favorite joke told by sardonic demons at the Gates of Hell. The Sons of Sceva tried to cast out demons without being under the authority of the Kingdom of God and the demons rose up within their possessed minion and gave them a good thrashing until they were bleeding and naked (see Acts 19:13-17). If you want the devil to get off your back, run for cover. Dwelling under the shadow of the Most High and coming under His nurturing protection happens when you are submitted. Then you can take authority over the demonic because you are under the authority of God's kingdom (see Luke 10:38).

Some folks quote the second half of James 4:7: *"Resist the devil and he will flee from you."* But they conveniently leave out the first part. You must be under authority to have authority. Submitting under authority is not about surrendering your dignity and kissing the ring of some narcissistic megalomaniac. Submission is about coming under the protection of authority. When you become an American citizen you must raise your right hand and swear allegiance to the Constitution of the United States of America. Once you agree to come under the governing authority, you are now under the protection of the military might of that nation.

In the eighth chapter of Matthew's gospel, a centurion came to Jesus and pleaded with Him to heal his servant. His servant was paralyzed and dreadfully tormented. When Jesus agreed to come to his home and heal him, the centurion answered and said, *"Lord, I am not worthy that you should come under my roof. But only speak a word, and my servant will be healed. For I also am a man under authority, having soldiers under me. And I say to this one, 'Go,' and he goes; and to another, 'Come,' and he comes; and to my servant, 'Do this,' and he does it" (Matthew 8:5-13).* Jesus marveled and praised the centurion for having great faith, and from that moment on his servant was healed.

Notice the centurion said that he was a man under authority and had soldiers under him. Why would Roman soldiers obey and respect a commander? At any time, they could rise up against him, overpower him, and select their own leader. They had no choice but to respect the authority of the centurion because he was under the authority of Rome. All the might and power of the Roman Empire backed up this centurion as he acted on Rome's behalf. If a soldier didn't obey, the entire military force of Rome would come crashing down on him. If you are under the authority of God, you can command demons to flee and they have to obey you. If they don't, then the entire force and power of the Kingdom of God comes crashing down on that demonic force. God and His kingdom back you up when you are acting within the boundaries of the Word of God.

The great faith of the centurion was linked to his understanding of authority and his honor for the authority of Jesus. Honor is huge in the Kingdom of God. It goes side by side with proper submission to authority. Show me what a person honors and I will show you his destiny. What you honor is what influences you and your decisions. Our faith is connected to how we honor the spiritual authority in our lives.

When Jesus went to His home town of Nazareth, He said, "*A prophet is not without honor except in his own country, among his own relatives, and in his own house" (Mark 6:4).* Then the text goes on to say: *"Now He could do no mighty work there, except that He laid His hands on a few sick people and healed them. And He marveled because of their unbelief. Then He went about the villages in a circuit, teaching" (Mark 6:5-6).*

The same Jesus that was amazed at the great faith of the centurion is marveling because of the unbelief in His home town of Nazareth. The working of miracles and the release of faith was very much connected to the honor given to Jesus, and the respect for His spiritual authority. They were saying that He was the *"son of Mary"* and they were offended at Him (Mark 6:2-3). In that culture, you referred to people as the son of the father, not the mother; for example, David Ben-Jesse, or David the son of Jesse. To call someone the son of the mother was to bring into question the fatherhood of the individual. In a small town, I'm sure the rumor got around that Mary was pregnant before she married Joseph. They were, in essence, saying, *"How dare that bastard son of Mary come here and teach us."* Wow...

If folks treated Jesus that way, do you think it's possible that people will treat spiritual authority that way today? (That is a rhetorical question, the answer is obvious.) Some people will tell me that they will only submit to Jesus. While that sounds noble on the surface, it stinks of rebellion. If you can't honor and submit to the human authority that God has placed in your life, how will you submit to God's authority? (Another rhetorical question.) If you can't love people that you can see, how will you love God whom you cannot see (see 1 John 4:20)? If you can't submit to legitimate spiritual authority on earth, how will you submit to the authority of heaven? (This is the paragraph of rhetorical questions.)

> *He who hears you hears Me, he who rejects you rejects Me, and he who rejects Me rejects Him who sent Me.*
> *— Luke 10:16*

It's very important that you honor and submit to the authority that God has placed over you. In the same way that the miracles of Jesus were cut off from the poor people of Nazareth, you will be cut off from the revelation and gifting of your leadership because of your dishonor. Have you ever heard people say, "I'm just not being fed anymore at that church." When people start talking along these lines, it's because they have lost respect for leadership. Whether it's justified or not, because of their dishonor they have been cut off from the revelation and virtue flowing from that ministry. We need to let God deal with our critical hearts or we will forfeit our promotion. When we avoid the dealings of God on our rebellious hearts, we bounce around from job to job and church to church, blaming everyone else for our dissatisfaction when we need only to look in the mirror. You are in a position to sow seeds of honor and submission towards your future right now. *"Whatever a man sows, that he will also reap" (see Galatians 6:7)*. You cannot reap a harvest where you have not sown. Begin sowing NOW for a harvest of honor and submission.

OBEY AUTHORITY THAT IT MAY GO WELL WITH YOU

> *Children, obey your parents in the Lord, for this is right. "Honor your father and mother," which is the first commandment*

> *with promise: "that it may be well with you and you may live long on the earth."*
> *— Ephesians 6:1-3*

I believe this scripture to have a two-fold meaning. The first is straightforward enough: Children need to honor and obey their parents. But when you look at the phrase, "*parents in the Lord,*" you are now talking about spiritual parents. The spiritual fathers and mothers of the church also need to be honored; "*that it may be well with you and you may live long on the earth.*"

The apostle Paul refers to himself as a spiritual father of the Corinthians: "*For though you might have ten thousand instructors in Christ, yet you do not have many fathers; for in Christ Jesus I have begotten you through the gospel*" (1 Corinthians 4:15). He didn't have a problem laying on the "guilt trip" to remind them to listen and follow his directives. He was their spiritual father; he had paternal rights to speak into their lives. He had to answer to God for their well-being.

I once was the Outreach Director of a growing church. I was interviewing a great guy to head up our Visitor Follow-up ministry. I loved this guy and had spoken into his life several times, even though he was an older man. When I found out he wasn't working, I had to tell him that I couldn't let him head a ministry until he found another job. He was in his mid-forties and had designed and built wood furniture for many years. The business was owned by his brother but the brother was closing it down. What could he do? Woodworking was the only real skill he thought he possessed for a successful career. Being in your mid-forties doesn't make it easy to start over.

I gave him some really hard advice. I told my friend to get an entry-level job, and that I believed in no time he would be in a supervisory role. He was very intelligent and someone who could handle responsibility; I was sure he would rise into management quickly.

Now it sometimes happens that after a while people become cynical in ministry. You know it's wrong, but it can happen. You give, what you believe to be great advice, but it seems that nine times out of ten people don't respect your advice and blow it off. So I was concerned that my friend wouldn't listen to me and stay on unemployment until it went dry, and then be left with nothing in the end.

A couple of weeks after speaking with my friend, I was walking through the local mall and was about to pass the Hot Pretzel stand. Lo and behold there he was working behind the counter wearing a goofy hot pretzel hat. "Would you like your pretzel plain or whole wheat? Would you like mustard or cheese on this salty hot pretzel?"

You know, it wasn't very long until he became the manager of that outlet. He made that store the most profitable in the state! Pretty soon they wanted him to be a district manager. He also headed our Greeter and Visitor Follow-up ministries. He was excellent, and everything he put his hands to prospered.

"Believe in the LORD your God, and you shall be established; believe His prophets, and you shall prosper" (2 Chronicles 20:20b). When you believe the Lord your God, you will be established. When you honor the advice of the prophets and preachers of the Lord, you will prosper. When you listen to the advice of spiritual fathers and mothers, it will be well with you.

When you humble yourself under the mighty hand of God, He will exalt you in due time. If you are stubbornly bent on a course of action and several mature leaders of your church are getting a check in their spirits about it, at the least, you should strongly consider your course.

Moses was the greatest Old Testament prophet. God spoke to him face to face, as a man speaks to his friend (see Numbers 33:11). He wrote the first five books of the Bible, the Pentateuch. This was the foundation of the entire Word of God. The Lord worked mighty signs and wonders through him such as the world had never seen. He called down the ten plagues of Egypt, and through him, the Lord split the Red Sea so the children of Israel could walk across on dry land. And after all of this, Moses' older brother and sister decided it was time for a regime change. *They* wanted to be the new leadership of Israel. (This is one of history's dumbest political coups.)

It's all recorded in Numbers chapter twelve. Aaron and Miriam found the right opportunity to make their move when old Moses married an Ethiopian woman. It wasn't illegal or wrong to marry a person from another ethnic group as long as that person was a convert to the Jewish religion. But playing on the general racism of their people, Aaron and Miriam criticized Moses and thought they would have the political leverage to stage an overthrow. (Did I mention how dumb this was? In what universe did they think this was a good idea?) God is not a politician. He doesn't take a vote or consult a polling committee to see if we agree with Him. He doesn't wet His finger and put it in the air to see what direction the political winds are blowing and then make decisions accordingly.

God's Kingdom is a theocracy, not a democracy. He is an all-wise, benevolent dictator; Moses was God's leader by divine appointment. The power and might of the Kingdom of God stood behind God's appointed man. Suddenly, God speaks and demands that all three of them come to the Tabernacle for a meeting:

> "Hear now My words:
> If there is a prophet among you,
> I, the LORD, make Myself known to him in a vision;
> I speak to him in a dream.
> Not so with My servant Moses;
> He is faithful in all My house.
> I speak with him face to face,
> Even plainly, and not in dark sayings;
> And he sees the form of the LORD.
> Why then were you not afraid
> To speak against My servant Moses?"
> So the anger of the LORD was aroused against them, and He departed. And when the cloud departed from above the tabernacle, suddenly Miriam became leprous, as white as snow. Then Aaron turned toward Miriam, and there she was, a leper.
> — Numbers 12:6-10

Miriam's leprosy caused her to be quarantined from the rest of the community. She was shut out of the camp for seven days. Let me ask you a question here. The leprosy, pain, and isolation that Miriam experienced, who caused it? The answer is that Miriam caused it! Miriam came against the leadership in a harsh way to do harm and was injured and isolated from the experience. Does this sound familiar? Some folks today contract spiritual leprosy. They have attacked leadership unjustly and are hurting and isolated. If you ask them, they would say that THEY are the victims of being abused by leadership. The truth is, they brought it on themselves by unjustly coming against leadership. They may tell you that they don't ever want to be part of another church, but in reality, they have spiritual leprosy. They are being quarantined by God because they are a cancer of rebellion to the body of Christ. That's NOT to say that there's not some legitimate hurting people out there, wounded by abusive leadership, folks that need to learn to trust again and be restored to the church. But some are victims of their own rebellion. When they come to their senses and repent, then their quarantine will be over and they will enter sweet fellowship with the body of Christ (see 2 Timothy 2:24-26). Obey and honor your fathers and mothers in the Lord that it may be well with you.

CONCLUSION

Obey your leaders and submit to their authority.
They keep watch over you as men who must give an account.
Obey them so that their work will be a joy, not a burden,
for that would be of no advantage to you.
— Hebrews 13:17 NIV

As you progress through your test of honor and submission to authority, let me clue you in on one more area of testing. There will be times when you will be forced to submit to a leader/boss that you deem as unfit to follow. Everything in you will loathe having to submit to this inferior being. You will no doubt out-qualify this individual in both training/education and experience. But somehow you feel that the malevolent universe has somehow chosen you to be the whipping boy for this idiot. Congratulations! You have now entered the "submission test" zone.

There will come another time when you will be the person that's in the lead. And guess what? There will be people under you more qualified. You will have to rely on the fact that God put you in that position. He anoints (enables) those He calls and chooses. You are going to want to sow many seeds of submission because there will come a day when you will need to harvest a crop of submission from your subordinates.

There was a time when I was asked to play lead guitar at a revival/renewal meeting. God was drawing people from out of the woodwork to these meetings. Each meeting was a full house. One night as I took the platform to play with the worship team, I spotted a familiar figure in the front row. It was a well-known guitar guru; we'll call him Gustavo. Gustavo knew riffs for his riffs. He knew musical scales from all over the world, Japanese scales, Indian scales and Hawaiian scales (if there is such a thing). His playing was clean, tasteful and ripping. If the game was to intimidate and dominate, Gustavo was the winner. I was sweating bullets knowing that I was about to be scrutinized by the master shredder.

Then an inner voice rose up inside me and said, "You're the one up here, not him." The Holy Spirit saw my plight and was reminding me that He had chosen me to play for this revival and not Gustavo. Although I was less qualified, I had to settle with the fact that I was "the man," and I knew THE MAN (Jesus). I settled into the confidence that God will anoint whom He chooses and calls. When you are playing under the Anointing of the Spirit, there is a glory in your tones. Sweet melodies flow that speak encouragement and touch the soul. After the meeting, Gustavo approached me and shook my hand. He complimented my playing and said that he was really caught up with God during the worship. This was God's greatest reward to me; to know that I was used to help facilitate a divine appointment between God and man. To be used to encourage another in Christ is a great feeling.

Please humble yourself and pass your test of submission. The body of Christ needs what you have to offer. Don't keep going around and around the mountain. Make your stand now. Determine to pass your test and move on to the high call of God. He is faithful to stay with you until the end. Your heavenly Father is determined to bring you to maturity.

> *Being confident of this very thing, that He who has begun a good work in you will complete it until the day of Jesus Christ.*
> *— Philippians 1:6*

Chapter 4

The Wilderness and The Promised Land

THE TEST OF LACK AND PROSPERITY

And you shall remember that the LORD your God led you all the way these forty years in the wilderness, to humble you and test you, to know what was in your heart, whether you would keep His commandments or not. So He humbled you, allowed you to hunger, and fed you with manna which you did not know nor did your fathers know, that He might make you know that man shall not live by bread alone; but man lives by every word that proceeds from the mouth of the LORD.
— *Deuteronomy 8:2-3*

The Wilderness is a place of stripping away. When all you have is God and His Word, you discover that God is all you really need. "*...that He might make you know that man shall not live by bread alone; but man lives by every word that proceeds from the mouth of the Lord.*" When all options have been exhausted and all that is left is a promise from God, that precious word from God becomes the hope of life itself. God's Word becomes more precious than gold. God and His Word become an anchor to your soul in the instability of the ever-shifting sands of life. It all comes down to raw faith; to knowing and trusting in the Lord. You CANNOT truly understand the freedom of dependency on God until everything is stripped away. Then the Lord shows you that He is all you need. When you possess God, everything for life and godliness is yours (see Matthew 6:33, 2 Peter 1:2-4). God spoke to Abram, *"Do not be afraid, Abram. I am your shield, your exceedingly great reward" (Genesis 15:1b).* The great "I AM" is your great reward in an insecure world. This truth is never realized until you reach a point where God and His word are all you have left. Embrace the Wilderness and stripping away of all false securities. For when neither poverty nor riches have a hold on you, then you have discovered riches beyond imagination; the secret of contentment. For if you have God, you have all you need and abound.

> *Not that I speak in regard to need, for I have learned in whatever state I am, to be content: I know how to be abased, and I know how to abound. Everywhere and in all things I have learned both to be full and to be hungry, both to abound and to suffer need. I can do all things through Christ who strengthens me.*
> *— Philippians 4:11-13*

I'm not promoting a vow of poverty; I'm advocating a total freedom from the trappings of materialism. Money and things will no longer rule you when you have been stripped of everything and find out that God will provide. You are now able to obey God and do things by faith that previously would have been unthinkable. If the love of money is the root of all kinds of evil (see 1 Timothy 6:10), shouldn't it stand to reason that God would want us free from dependency on this world system? Knowing that God will supply any endeavor to which

He calls you is very liberating. The Wilderness will liberate us from enslavement to Egypt so that we may be truly free (see John. 8:36).

I once went through a very discouraging time as a pastor. Some people that I loved very much had left the church and were slandering my family. It was very, very painful. I had never before experienced that level of personal betrayal. I was on my knees in the empty church one afternoon crying out to the Lord. I had made up my mind to quit ministry altogether. I figured that I had too much self-dignity to allow myself and my family to go through this. I had decided that I would go back to sales work and make a pile of money. After all, I didn't sign up to be a doormat for people. As I wallowed in my self-pity, I was suddenly overwhelmed by the presence of God. I felt directed to Psalm 16:5-6, "*O LORD, You are the portion of my inheritance and my cup; You maintain my lot. The lines have fallen to me in pleasant places; yes, I have a good inheritance.*"

God was very profoundly expressing to me the privilege He had given to me. Not only was He my great reward, but ministry was my inheritance. I can't tell you how much that meant to me at the time. The lines had fallen to me in pleasant places; yes, I have a good inheritance. No one can take my inheritance, and I would never again be tempted to squander it because of the fickle affections of people. In some ways, abandonment and betrayal worked for my good. Because of that stripping away, I can love more freely. It doesn't matter what people do, I have a sure inheritance. When you are in a secure place in your relationship with God, you can love without fear.

Only by going through the Wilderness can you truly appreciate all of life's most profound and simple blessings. How can I rejoice in God's abundance unless I have experienced lack? Like a blind man who sees the beauty of a sunset painted with majestic orange, red and magenta for the first time, all the colors of life become richer and fuller when you have gone through your Wilderness. You are never completely free until you realize that God is all you need.

Don't get me wrong, God wants to bless you with fulfilling relationships and material blessings, but everything must be in its proper place and order. We run into trouble when we look too much to relationships, stuff, and goals to ultimately fulfill us; they are incapable in themselves of making you happy. When God is first place and everything else is in proper order then there is balance, and life is enjoyable. The Wilderness test puts things in their right perspective; without it, we cannot keep God's blessings in proper poise. No one who comes to Christ escapes going through the Wilderness test. There is only one way to get to your Promised Land, and that is through the Wilderness. The Wilderness is a preparation time for good things to come. In the harsh, arid desert environment of the Wilderness, the roots of faith are forced to bore downward into refreshing artesian springs. No more will you be dependent on outward circumstances to remain satiated in your soul. You have found a river that never runs dry.

> *...who led you through that great and terrible wilderness, in which were fiery serpents and scorpions and thirsty land where there was no water; who brought water for you out of the flinty rock; who fed you in the wilderness with*

> manna, which your fathers did not know, that He might
> humble you and **that He might test you, to do
> you good in the end.**
> — Deuteronomy 8:15-16

THE WILDERNESS TEACHES OBEDIENCE

> Then it came to pass, when Pharaoh had let the people go,
> that God did not lead them by way of the land of the
> Philistines, although that was near; for God said, "Lest perhaps
> the people change their minds when they see war,
> and return to Egypt." So God led the people around
> by way of the wilderness of the Red Sea. And the children
> of Israel went up in orderly ranks out of the land of Egypt.
> — Exodus 13:17-18

It was only a few weeks' journey to the land of Canaan, but they had to have time to get organized and coalesce as a nation before they faced the prospect of war. There was no way to avoid going through the Wilderness. It would be two years in the Wilderness before they came to Kadesh, the threshold of the Promised Land. Before they could begin their conquest of the land, they had to journey to Mount Sinai and become established in the laws and ways of God.

> And now, Israel, what does the LORD your God require of you,
> but to fear the LORD your God, to walk in all His ways and to
> love Him, to serve the LORD your God with all your heart and
> with all your soul, and to keep the commandments of the LORD
> and His statutes which I command you today for your good?
> — Deuteronomy 10:12-13

Isn't this like the Christian faith? First, we are delivered from the oppression and slavery of this world system (Egypt), and then we must go into the Wilderness to learn faith and obedience. We must be trained in the Word of God and learn how to apply the promises of God to our lives. I've heard it said, and I believe it, that Egypt is the land of "not enough," the Wilderness is the land of "just enough," and the Promised Land of Canaan is the land of "more than enough." Before we can experience the victory and bounty of the Promised Land we must be tested so that we can appreciate and hold the blessings. What good is a land of plenty if your character is so bad that you can't maintain and hold onto those blessings?

After two years, the children of Israel camped at the gateway of the Promised Land, coming from the Wilderness way. It was a place called Kadesh Barnea (see Deuteronomy 9:23). Here Moses sent out twelve spies to assess the land, and ten of them came back with an "evil report" of the land (see Numbers 13:31-32 KJV). Their time in the wilderness could have ended right there at the two-year mark, but they failed to view the strongholds of the land with the eyes of faith. A mind that's not renewed in the Word of God will have a diminished perspective (see Romans 12:2). Even though Joshua and Caleb tried to persuade the other ten spies and the nation to believe God and possess the land, it was to no avail. Here is a good lesson: If you don't renew your mind to your new identity in Christ as a child of the King and co-heir with Christ, you will not be able to see the victorious living that Christ purchased for you.

Because of the bad testimony of the land given by the ten unbelieving spies, Israel was disobedient and unable to possess the land by faith. God brought them into discipline by making them wander the wilderness for 38 more years, a total of forty years; a year for every day the spies were on their mission to scout out the land (see Numbers 14:33-34). That generation perished in the Wilderness, never realizing their full destiny in Christ. At the end of forty years, the children of Israel found themselves right back at Kadesh Barnea, ready again to invade the Promised Land. They came right back to their place of disobedience until they got it right.

Here's the thing: How long you stay in the Wilderness depends on you. Your stay in the Wilderness can be 2 years or 40 years, it's all dependent upon your faith and obedience. Faith and obedience go hand in hand. You cannot truly be obedient without believing the promise. When you are disobedient, you're forced to wander until you are truly repentant. God will bring us right back to the place of disobedience that kept us from progressing. If you don't want to stay in the Wilderness, then you must overcome your area of testing. This area of testing may be different from one person to the next. Folks seem to get to the juncture in their Christian walk where there is some major issue that must be overcome right before a major promotion. With some folks, it could be tobacco or abusing alcohol. For others it could be an anger problem, or an offense; greed or selfish ambition. Whatever God is putting His finger on in your life, it's not worth forfeiting your promised land. I've seen people wander for years at the very threshold of something awesome, only to stubbornly continue holding onto some fleshly thing.

> *"Now the just shall live by faith; but if anyone draws back, My soul has no pleasure in him."*
> *But we are not of those who draw back to perdition, but of those who believe to the saving of the soul.*
> *— Hebrews 10:38-39*

THE WILDERNESS TEACHES US TO OVERCOME IN OBSCURITY

So the child grew and became strong in spirit, and was in the desert till the day of his manifestation to Israel.
— Luke 1:80

There is a hidden place of preparation before manifestation into public ministry. It was in the solitude of desert places that John the Baptist became strong in spirit. You and I must go through our hidden times; in God's perfect timing He releases us into full view. A hidden place is a place of protection. When you come-out of stealth mode, you also become a target. As much as we want a coming out party, becoming a blip on the devil's radar can be hazardous if you haven't been prepared. John the Baptist lost his head over this deal; don't lose yours by coming out of hiding before God's release.

Jesus was led by the Spirit into the Wilderness before His ministry was launched. If it was important for Jesus to go through the Wilderness, then for sure it's important for you and me.

Immediately the Spirit drove Him into the wilderness. And He was there in the wilderness forty days, tempted by Satan, and was with the wild beasts; and the angels ministered to Him.
— Mark 1:12-13

One cannot help but notice that there is significance to Jesus being in the wilderness for 40 days. The number 40 appears in the Bible 146 times. In the study of Bible numerology, the number 40 symbolizes a period of testing, trial or probation. It represents the completion of a cycle. The life of Moses is divided into three 40-year periods. 40 years being a prince

The Wilderness and The Promised Land

of Egypt, 40 years in the Midian wilderness, and 40 years as the mighty prophet, deliverer and lawgiver. There is a cycle of time that must be completed in our Wilderness experience. God will box you in so that you must fulfill your cycle. There are only three ways out: you die there having never reached your potential, you totally backslide and forsake God, or you wait until your release.

When I was in my early twenties I traveled in a Christian Rock band, and we had achieved nominal notoriety. When the band broke up I took a job as a cook in a local restaurant. I went from signing autographs to flipping hamburgers and flapjacks. I kept telling the folks that I was only there for a short time, and once our band was pulled back together we would be back on the road. I ended up working there for nine years… just let that sink in.

During that time I was not idle; I did a lot of volunteer ministry in my local church, I put myself through a Bible institute and a Bachelor's degree program, I worked my buns off, and basically grew up. It wasn't until I was married that God started to release me from my job as a cook.

Oh, I tried to escape my Wilderness experience, but to no avail. I tried applying for all kinds of work but God sabotaged my efforts. I remember when I was offered a manager's position in a competing restaurant down the road and the Lord witnessed in my heart that I would not be blessed if I took the job. Although I couldn't see what God was doing at the time, as I look back I can see clearly. The Lord needed me in a stable spot to get me through some schooling and to work some maturity into my life.

Being a steady stable person, able to achieve long and short-term goals, speaks very highly of one's character. Stay with it; slow and steady is better than fast and reckless.

We see how Jesus was led by the Holy Spirit into the Wilderness. If Jesus had to go through a Wilderness experience before He was used of God, so will you. The awesome thing about Jesus is that after He came out of the Wilderness, the Gospel of Luke has this to say: "*Then Jesus returned in the power of the Spirit to Galilee, and news of Him went out through all the surrounding region. And He taught in their synagogues, being glorified by all*" *(Luke 4:14-15)*. Jesus came out of the Wilderness powerful in the Spirit. You and I need to be tested and refined so that more power can be released through our lives.

> *But may the God of all grace, who called us to His eternal glory by Christ Jesus, after you have suffered a while, perfect, establish, strengthen, and settle you. To Him be the glory and the dominion forever and ever. Amen.*
> *— 1 Peter 5:10-11*

Our heavenly Father's ultimate goal is to make us fit for the Master's use. Your testing will perfect, establish, strengthen and settle you. God receives great glory from stable lives that are a good witness to the world. There is nothing that God can't pull you through if you can stand the pull. Hang on and don't give up. Stay with it, trust and obey; God has a desired end. He knows what He is doing. He's been in the character-building business for quite a while now. There is a Promised Land on the other side of your Wilderness experience; keep plugging away.

Whatever you do, don't get restless and take matters into your own hands. You may be tempted to think God is taking too long and start looking for a shortcut. Remember, you can be in the Wilderness for 2 years or 40 years, it's all up to you. You can't outflank the Lord. You will end up back at the same test you tried to circumvent in your self-deceived cleverness.

THE PROMISED LAND

And you shall remember the LORD your God, for it is He who gives you power to get wealth, that He may establish His covenant which He swore to your fathers, as it is this day.
— Deuteronomy 8:18

There is a land of plenty for the people of God. I sometimes hear preachers talk with disdain about the "Prosperity Gospel." I never understood that, because if we are not teaching that a life surrendered to Christ will elevate you to abundant provision then what are we preaching? "Come to Christ and expect no hope. Die sick, poor and miserable."?

I was on a short-term mission trip to Peru and the fella I was teamed up with was paranoid of the "Prosperity Gospel." As he preached through a translator he would say things like, "If you come to Christ there may not be any change in your circumstances." Even the translator rebuked him, and rightly so. God has abundant provision for all His children; He is a good provider.

And God is able to make all grace abound toward you, that you, always having all sufficiency in all things, may have an abundance for every good work.
— 2 Corinthians 9:8

God's grace provides all sufficiency in ALL THINGS. And for what purpose? So that you have an abundance for every good work He has called you to. I like to challenge people along these lines, "If money was not an option, what would you do with your life? If money was not an option, what would you do for God?" Let's dream big and expect big! God has a special work for you to do. His grace has downloaded the faith in your spirit to secure the resources to accomplish the task.

> *Beloved, I pray that you may prosper in all things and be in health, just as your soul prospers.*
> — 3 John 2

This New Testament verse is crystal clear as to God's will concerning prosperity. God wants you to prosper in all ways; financially, socially, mentally, spiritually and physically. In every dynamic possible, God desires His children to advance. The key is the prosperity of the soul. Our soul prospers as we renew our minds and walk out the truth we know. As the Spirit of the Lord washes over our wounded soul, bringing the healing virtue of heaven, we are free to prosper.

When we consider typology in the Old Testament, what does the Promised Land represent? Many older commentaries tell us that it represents heaven. Crossing the Jordan into the Promised Land is passing the threshold of death. I disagree that the Promised Land represents heaven for several reasons: Will we be at war in heaven? Will there be a chance that we will fall away from God by learning the customs of the nations around us and forfeit our blessings? NO!

The Promised Land represents our place of victory and bounty. In the Wilderness we learn to live by faith and overcome the wicked one. The foundations of the Word of God are etched into our souls with a diamond pen. We emerge from the obscure thirsty Wilderness as spiritual warriors.

The only drawback of the Promised Land is that your testing does not end. No, you haven't arrived yet. In the Wilderness you are tested with lack, now you will be tested with prosperity. I can hear you saying right now, "Bring it on! I would love to be tested with prosperity!" "If a man must be tested, I'd rather be tested with prosperity than lack." True enough, but there are pitfalls. The big two are pride and greed. Let's talk about pride first.

We must remember that it is the Lord who gives us the power to create wealth. We can't allow ourselves to claim that we made it completely on our own. Everyone gets help, whether it's training, an inheritance, good advice, or whatever, it all comes from God. Opportunities and the strength to work hard come from God. There is a business and administrative anointing available that you must claim. It's your inheritance. God must establish the covenant that He swore to your fathers.

Abram was wealthy: *Genesis 13:2 - Abram was very rich in livestock, in silver, and in gold.*

Isaac was wealthy: *Genesis 26:12-14 - Then Isaac sowed in that land, and reaped in the same year a hundredfold; and the LORD blessed him. The man began to prosper, and continued prospering until he became very prosperous; for he had possessions of flocks and possessions of herds and a great number of servants. So the Philistines envied him.*

Jacob was wealthy: *Genesis 32:10 - I am not worthy of the least of all the mercies and of all the truth which You have shown Your servant; for I crossed over this Jordan with my staff, and now I have become two companies.*

I could cite example after example. *"The blessing of the Lord makes one rich, and He adds no sorrow with it" (Proverbs 10:22)*. The riches that King Solomon is talking about here is not just spiritual riches, it's filthy lucre, it's cold hard cash, it's stuff, lots of stuff. When riches come God's way and in God's timing, there is no sorrow with it. You will know how to handle it and it won't handle you.

> Command those who are rich in this present age not to be haughty, nor to trust in uncertain riches but in the living God, who gives us richly all things to enjoy. Let them do good, that they be rich in good works, ready to give, willing to share, storing up for themselves a good foundation for the time to come, that they may lay hold on eternal life.
> — 1 Timothy 6:17-19

I just want to bring some balance to the "Prosperity Gospel." In the above passage, God does not have a problem with rich people. He has a problem with pride and haughtiness. He also has a problem with not sharing some of the bounty that God has blessed them with. Being rich is not a more blessed state than poverty, it IS more responsibility though.

The next temptation with wealth is greed. John Rockefeller was asked once, "How much more do you need to be satisfied?" His response, "Just a little more." How much does a person really need to live comfortably? When is having abundance for every good work not enough?

I haven't heard too many sermons on covetousness and greed. In our debt-ridden society, I don't think it would be popular to preach about living within your means. If your debt is ten times greater than your net worth, could it be that you have a greed problem? Greed is not just a trapping of the wealthy. Running after stuff to the point that we put our children's children in debt is NOT leaving a good inheritance. We need to be retrained in economic empowerment so that we can leverage debt properly and not be swept away blindly by our culture of indebtedness. The Bible is NOT against indebtedness. Poor debt management IS portrayed in the Bible as a lack of wisdom.

> *The LORD will open to you His good treasure, the heavens,*
> *to give the rain to your land in its season, and to bless*
> *all the work of your hand. You shall lend to many nations,*
> ***but you shall not borrow.***
> *— Deuteronomy 28:12*

> *The rich rules over the poor,*
> *And the borrower is servant to the lender.*
> *— Proverbs 22:7*

> *The wicked borrows and does not repay,*
> *But the righteous shows mercy and gives.*
> *— Psalms 37:21*

> *Let no debt remain outstanding, except the continuing*
> *debt to love one another, for he who loves his fellowman*
> *has fulfilled the law.*
> *— Romans 13:8 NIV*

We must always remember to seek God first in all major financial decisions. If He is our first passion, and we are in hot pursuit of His kingdom, then all things will be added (See Matthew 6:33, Deuteronomy 28:14). Maintaining proper order will protect us from the greed trap. When stuff and money usurp God on the throne of life, destruction is forthcoming.

What we need to do is define "greed." Having ambition

and wanting to be successful is not wrong. Wanting to be prosperous is not wrong either. It's when you are willing to compromise your faith and do things that are unethical that you step into the greed zone. It's when you can't obey the call of God because you are greedy for more that you have a problem. When DO you have enough money to be able to preach the Gospel? Don't let a lack of money be an excuse for not obeying God.

> *Now he who received seed among the thorns is he who hears the word, and the cares of this world and the deceitfulness of riches choke the word, and he becomes unfruitful. But he who received seed on the good ground is he who hears the word and understands it, who indeed bears fruit and produces: some a hundredfold, some sixty, some thirty.*
> *— Matthew 13:22-23*

Don't let the *lack* of the Wilderness or the *prosperity* of the Promised Land keep you from becoming mega fruitful. You must go through your Wilderness before you reach your Promised Land. When you learn that God is all you need, poverty or riches make no difference. Poverty or riches will have no hold on you. Your joy comes from your relationship with God in whatever circumstance you are in. The important thing is that you stay tight with the Lord. He is all you need.

> *Not that I speak in regard to need, for I have learned in whatever state I am, to be content: I know how to be abased, and I know how to abound. Everywhere and in all things I have learned both to be full and to be hungry, both to abound and to suffer need. I can do all things through Christ who strengthens me.*
> *— Philippians 4:11-13*

Chapter 5

Approved or Disqualified

APPROVAL HAPPENS AFTER PASSING YOUR TEST

But He knows the way that I take; **When He has tested me,**
I shall come forth as gold.
— Job 23:10

The refining pot is for silver and the furnace for gold,
*But **the Lord tests the hearts.***
— Proverbs 17:3

You and I must be tested. Before we can be entrusted with more we must be tested with little. Before you can pass a college course and advance to the next grade, you must be tested. Have you grasped the lessons? Have you grown in your skills?

In karate, the student is drilled over and over until muscle memory is honed to a sharp point. Repetition is the mother of skill. At first you must think and force your body into certain movements and actions. The muscles, joints and even some bones become sore from the conditioning. After time and exercise, the body responds almost mindlessly. When a punch is thrown at you, you block, chamber your fist and strike back with an economy of motion that utilizes power from your legs and hips. It's a conditioned response from hours of training and repetition. One well-placed strike will end the conflict. When I was tested for my first black belt, the testing board didn't just want to see the complex black belt forms (katas) I knew. They wanted to see the first basic form I ever learned, done at a black belt level. Have the stances been perfected? Is there a fluidity of motion? Has the student mastered swiveling the hip? By the time the student has reached black belt level, that first form should have been practiced a thousand times. Bruce Lee once said, "I fear not the man who has practiced 10,000 kicks once, but I fear the man who has practiced one kick 10,000 times."

It's the general consensus in the martial arts world that only 1% or less of all students who begin training will achieve a black belt. A black belt is still only entrance level into the martial arts world, it means that a beginner has achieved solid fundamental skills. Of all black belts, only 5-10% will go on to achieve a second one. Karate is a constant quest for improvement and perfection. And since perfection can never be achieved, the journey never ends.

If we take the karate illustration and apply it to a Christian's journey to spiritual maturity, what is the percentage of believers in Christ that reach full maturity? How many never advance from the lower ranks? How many never exercise their faith to mountain moving levels? How many will discipline themselves to read and study God's word on a daily basis until they become mighty in the scriptures? Salvation is a free gift, but rewards and advancements must be earned. There will be a test and the courts of heaven will make a ruling; you will either be **approved** for promotion or **disqualified**.

THERE IS AN APPROVAL

> *Blessed is the man who endures temptation; for when he has been **approved**, he will receive the crown of life which the Lord has promised to those who love Him.*
> *— James 1:12*

> *But as we have been **approved** by God to be entrusted with the gospel, even so we speak, not as pleasing men, but God who tests our hearts.*
> *— 1 Thessalonians 2:4*

I love the sound of that word "approved." Once I was standing in front of the cashier at the grocery store and after my debit/credit card was swiped, the little screen read, "APPROVED." Before thinking I yelled out, "YES, I am approved!" Several people stopped and stared. The cashier replied sardonically, "I'm glad that meant so much to you." I told her that words of affirmation are my love language. This did not help the awkwardness of the moment. I'm sure I hit about a 9.5 on her weirdo meter.

When I think of the approval from God after I have passed my test, I think of a big hand from heaven reaching down and stamping me on my forehead, "APPROVED." If there is an approval rating rewarded to me when I pass my test, there is a "disqualified" ruling when I fail. Only when I pass my tests will I be approved for reward and promotion.

> *Blessed (happy, to be envied) is the man who is patient under **trial** and stands up under **temptation**, for when he has stood*

> *the test and been **approved**, he will receive [the victor's] crown*
> *of life which God has promised to those who love Him.*
> *— James 1:12 AMP*

In James 1:12, the Bible says, "*Blessed is the man who endures temptation.*" The Greek word translated into the English word "*temptation*" in the above verse is "*peirasmos*" (Strong's #3986); it means to put to the test, a trial or affliction. This word is used for either a trial/hardship, or a solicitation/temptation to sin. A trial can definitely lead to wrongdoing (temptation) if not handled right. This Greek word is also used in 1 Corinthians 10:13, "*No temptation (trial) has overtaken you but such as is common to man...*". God is faithful and will not allow us to be tempted (tried) beyond what we can bear. I love the way James 1:12 includes both words "trial" and "temptation" in the Amplified translation. God has the grace for you to pass every trial, test, and temptation! In fact, He won't even allow a trial to come to your life that you can't handle. With the Lord's help, guidance, and support you and I can handle anything that life can throw at us.

> *I have strength for all things in Christ Who empowers me*
> *[I am ready for anything and equal to anything through Him*
> *Who infuses inner strength into me; I am self-sufficient*
> *in Christ's sufficiency].*
> *— Philippians 4:13 AMP*

PROMOTION COMES FROM GOD

You must always remember that God is the one who promotes and NOT MAN. Promotion can come through men, but God is the ultimate decision-maker. This is a good thing. Christians should be the most diligent and faithful workers on the planet, they work for God. You don't need an overabundance of pats on the back, or constant affirmation from people. You work for God.

> *Bondservants, obey in all things your masters according to the flesh, not with eyeservice, as men-pleasers, but in sincerity of heart, fearing God. And whatever you do, do it heartily, as to the Lord and not to men, knowing that* **from the Lord you will receive the reward** *of the inheritance; for you serve the Lord Christ. But he who does wrong will be repaid for what he has done, and there is no partiality.*
> — Colossians 3:22-25

Whatever you do, do it heartily as unto the Lord and not to men. When the above verse tells us not to give eyeservice as men-pleasers, it's talking about doing things just to be seen by people. It's great when people see how awesome you are, but how do you perform when no one is looking? What are you like in private? Will you work hard for God when no one will acknowledge it? When you feel you're not getting the credit or promotion you deserve, talk to God about it. He will give you wisdom and perspective for your situation (see James 1:5). Promotion comes from God.

> *He raises the poor out of the dust, and lifts the needy out of the ash heap, That He may seat him with princes— With the princes of His people. He grants the barren woman a home, Like a joyful mother of children. Praise the Lord!*
> — Psalms 113:7-9

> *Now therefore, thus shall you say to My servant David, 'Thus says the Lord of hosts: "I took you from the sheepfold, from following the sheep, to be ruler over My people, over Israel. And I have been with you wherever you have gone, and have cut off*

> *all your enemies from before you, and have made you a great name, like the name of the great men who are on the earth."*
> *— II Samuel 7:8-9*

> *Let them shout for joy and be glad, who favor my righteous cause; And let them say continually, "Let the Lord be magnified, Who has pleasure in the prosperity of His servant."*
> *— Psalms 35:27*

The Lord takes pleasure in your prospering. He gets glory when you are fruitful and progressing. He can give you divine favor. God's favor can open doors that will blow your mind. When I worked as a sales manager for a small company, I would pray for God's favor and declare *Psalm 5:12:* "*For you, Oh Lord, will bless the righteous; with favor You will surround him as with a shield.*" Every year, for three years in a row, I single-handedly doubled the revenue of the company. God's divine favor will bring outrageous promotion. This is why we must look to God for promotion and not man. Only God can give this kind of favor.

> ***The Lord was with Joseph, and he was a successful man;*** *and he was in the house of his master the Egyptian. And his master saw that the Lord was with him and that **the Lord made all he did to prosper in his hand. So Joseph found favor in his sight, and served him.*** *Then he made him overseer of his house, and all that he had he put under his authority.*
> *— Genesis 39:2-4*

GOD'S JUDGMENTS ARE IN THE EARTH NOW

At some point there is a judgment, or ruling of God, and after we have stood the test and been approved we will receive a reward and/or advancement. When we think of the judgment of God, we sometimes automatically think of fire and brimstone. We think of some epic disaster of biblical proportions poured out into the earth by a wrathful deity. This is only one aspect of God's judgments on the earth. And why is this the only side of God that some may know? As if God sits around bored with His finger on the "smite" button waiting for someone to mess up. Is there more to the judgments of God than just visualizing Him exacting vengeance on His enemies? I think that most of the time God doesn't have to directly judge us. The weight of our own sin carries its own judgment and negative consequences. I think the sovereign Lord spends more time restraining us from ourselves and rescuing us from reaping fully what our sins deserve, than He looks for ways to punish us.

The judgment of God is also a ruling. Besides the future judgments of God, His judgments are in the earth now. *"When I choose the proper time, I will judge uprightly" (Psalm 75:2).* At the appointed time He will make a ruling on your case. For a person to be tested and approved there must be a ruling. In the majestic courts of heaven, rulings are made. Your case is presented before the judge of all the earth. Books are opened and arguments are heard. Your court-appointed advocate is Jesus Christ. The prosecuting attorney is the accuser of the brethren, Satan. Thank God that we have the wisest lawyer in town (see 1 John 2:1). God's judgments are now and in the future.

He is the LORD our God; His judgments are in all the earth.
— 1 Chronicles 16:14

Once I went through a very hard trial. I experienced a romantic failure and was left heartbroken. A bad break-up and all the rejection, low self-worth, and emotional baggage that goes with it is not to be belittled. I've known people who were suicidal after a failed romantic relationship. One evening I was home alone, on my knees crying out to the Lord, and I went into a vision. It was like a portal was opened and I could see into the throne room of heaven. Jesus Himself fell on His knees and began interceding for me on the steps leading up to the throne. I was so blown away by the fact that I was valued enough to merit the Son of God's prayers that I just broke down and wept. I mean, I understood theologically that Jesus was my advocate and intercessor, but then I really understood what that meant (see 1 Timothy 2:5, Romans 8:27). It was shortly after this encounter that I met my wife to be.

> *Therefore He is also able to save to the uttermost those who come to God through Him, since He always lives to make intercession for them.*
> *— Hebrews 7:25*

THE FUTURE JUDGMENTS OF GOD

> *And as it is appointed for men to die once, but after this the judgment.*
> *— Hebrews 9:27*

> *Now as he reasoned about righteousness, self-control, and the judgment to come, Felix was afraid and answered, "Go away for now; when I have a convenient time I will call for you."*
> *— Acts 24:25*

There are judgments now, in this life, and judgments in the future. If we are serving the Lord with sincerity of heart, we do not have to be afraid of any judgment (see Acts 24:25, 1 John 4:17-19). Our sins have been judged at the cross. Our future in heaven has already been determined when we put our faith in Christ and live for Him. Any negative judgment I am referring to for the Christian would be in the form of chastisement/discipline now, in this life. Even if God does chastise us, it is for our own good.

> *For if we would judge ourselves, we would not be judged. But when we are judged, we are chastened by the Lord, that we may not be condemned with the world.*
> *— I Corinthians 11:31-32*

We have been saved from the wrath of God (see 1 Thessalonians 5:9, Ephesians 5:6-7). All judgment, now and in the future, has been committed to the Son of God. He alone is the perfect judge. Because He is God, His judgment is perfectly just; because He is man, He can identify with human frailties (see Romans 2:16).

> *For the Father judges no one, but has committed all judgment to the Son, that all should honor the Son just as they honor the Father. He who does not honor the Son does not honor the Father who sent Him.*
> *— John 5:22-23*

> *By me princes rule, and nobles, all the judges of the earth.*
> *— Proverbs 8:16*

> *The Lord makes poor and makes rich; He brings low and lifts up. He raises the poor from the dust and lifts the beggar from the ash heap, to set them among princes and make them inherit the throne of glory. For the pillars of the earth are the Lord's, and He has set the world upon them.*
> *— I Samuel 2:7-8*

Here is a list of the judgments of God. How does this help you understand promotion you ask? You must always remember that God promotes and not man; He is the judge of all the earth.

- **God's providential judgments** in the earth now: *"Far be it from You to do such a thing as this, to slay the righteous with the wicked, so that the righteous should be as the wicked; far be it from You!* **Shall not the Judge of all the earth do right?"** *(Genesis 18:25).* The courts of heaven are open and God is actively bringing divine justice and judgments to the earth (see 1 Chronicles 6:14, Proverbs 11:31, 1 Timothy 4:8).
- **The believer's self-judgment:** (see 1 Corinthians 11:31-32, 2 Corinthians 15:5, Hebrews 12:11) If we would judge ourselves, we would not be judged. We are to change and grow. Conforming to the truth of the Word of God is a process. If we resist and do not yield, things will get to the point where God steps in and disciplines us. This judgment is so important and so often overlooked. Through the grace of God and the indwelling power of the Holy Spirit, you can overcome.
- **The Judgment Seat of Christ** for believers: (see Romans 14:10-13, 1 Corinthians 3:11-17, 2 Corinthians 5:6-10) The Judgment seat of Christ is solely a Judgment for Christians. It is a future judgment not to determine whether a person goes to heaven or hell, but to determine rewards. As a Christian, you have been saved from eternal hell and the wrath of God, but there is reward for the faithful overcomers.

- **The Judgment of the Nations:** (see Matthew 25:31-46) This is a future judgment that will take place at the end of the Tribulation (the last seven years of this age). When Jesus returns, He will judge the living nations that are left. He will separate the sheep nations from the goats, and determine who enters the Millennial Kingdom (see Revelation 20-21).
- **The Great White Throne Judgment:** (see Revelation 20:11-15) This is a judgment for all the unrighteous dead. Books will be opened, and all those not found in the Book of Life will be cast into the lake of fire.

APPROVAL AND REWARDS

*But without faith it is impossible to please Him, for he who comes to God must believe that He is, and that **He is a rewarder of those who diligently seek Him.***
— Hebrews 11:6

Now that we have considered the judgments, let's consider the rewards; the rewards now, and in the life to come. *"...for when he has been approved, he will receive the crown of life which the Lord has promised to those who love Him"* (James 1:12b).

The Crown of Life is the ultimate reward; it's the fullness of eternal life. There will be no greater reward than to inherit eternity basking in the presence of God. To enjoy Him, and the pure love and accepting atmosphere of heaven, and ultimately the New Jerusalem, New Heavens, and New Earth, this will be THE great adventure.

Besides the reward of life eternal, there is another application to receiving the Crown of Life. When you have made it to the other side of tremendous suffering and a trial, there is a reward of more of the abundant life of Christ (see John 10:10). There is the reward of more life now and there is a special category of reward for those who go through unconscionable misery in this life. The only other time the "*Crown of Life*" is mentioned is in Revelation 2:10-11: "*Do not fear any of those things which you are about to suffer. Indeed, the devil is about to throw some of you into prison, that you may be tested, and you will have tribulation for ten days. Be faithful until death, and I will give you* **the crown of life**. *He who has an ear, let him hear what the Spirit says to the churches. He who overcomes shall not be hurt by the second death.*"

This special category of reward for those who go through great afflictions is called the "Crown of Life." If you and I are ever called to martyrdom for Christ, there will not only be a special grace to go through it, but a special reward. The point I'm trying to make clear is that God's reward is not just for the sweet by and by, but also for the here and now. Promised rewards have a twofold application; they can be realized both now and in the world to come.

If the righteous will be recompensed on the earth,
how much more the ungodly and the sinner.
— Proverbs 11:31

For bodily exercise profits a little, but godliness is profitable
for all things, ***having promise of the life that now is***
and of that which is to come.
— 1 Timothy 4:8

No trial or suffering goes unnoticed by the King of Kings. He identifies very personally with the suffering of His children. Jesus told Saul, when on the road to Damascus to persecute Christians, "*Saul, Saul, why do you persecute ME?*" *(Acts 9:4)*. God told Moses: *And the LORD said; "I have surely seen the oppression of My people who are in Egypt, and have heard their cry because of their taskmasters, for I know their sorrows"* *(Exodus 3:7-8)*. The Hebrew word for "know" is "yada" which means to *know intimately*. The last word in that verse is "sorrows" and can be translated as "pains." God's love for us is so intimate and profound that He suffers with us; like a loving parent suffers when their children suffer.

These are good things to keep in mind when you are tempted to think that God doesn't care. This is the same God who sent His Only Son to die in one of the most brutal deaths ever conceived by evil imaginations. He did it because He loves us and takes human suffering very personally. Jesus died vicariously for our sins so that we would be rescued from the apex of suffering eternal separation from His love, in a place of endless despair and burning torment; Hell, and the wrath of Almighty God (see 1 Thessalonians 5:9, Revelation 20:14-15).

God is a rewarder of those who diligently serve Him (see Hebrews 11:6, Matthew 25:21). He has promised great reward for the persecuted (see Matthew 5:11-12). Could it be that's why the apostles were happy to be permitted to suffer for His name (see Acts 5:41)? Perhaps that is why James tells us to count it all joy when we fall into various trials (see James 1:2). In the Book of Revelation, at the end of every letter to the seven churches is a promised reward "*To him who overcomes…*" (see Revelation 2-3); we can endure by looking to the promised reward. It is said of Moses, "*...esteeming the reproach of Christ greater riches than the treasures of Egypt; for he looked to the reward*" *(see Hebrews 11:26).*

The following are categories of rewards that are given to those who pass their tests and are approved:

- **The Crown of Life:** (see James 1:12, Revelation 2:10) A special reward for those who endure great suffering and persecution. Also a reward of more of the (Zoe) life of God in this life.
- **The Imperishable Crown:** (see 1 Corinthians 9:24-27) A reward for those who practiced great self-denial. I believe this applies to those who overcome addictions and learn to live in the self-control of the Holy Spirit (see Galatians 5:22-23). Perseverance and self-discipline will result in freedom from addictions in this life and a special reward in the next.
- **The Crown of Glory:** (see 1 Peter 5:1-4) A category of reward for faithful Pastors and leaders. There will also be a reward in this life for those who overcome and are approved. There will be a greater glory upon their life and ministry.
- **The Crown of Righteousness:** (see 2 Timothy 4:7-8) A special reward for those who long for and are watchful for Christ's coming. It's interesting to note that the hope of His coming has a purifying effect (see 1 John 3:3). The second coming of Christ must be vigilantly taught for the body of Christ to remain pure.
- **The Crown of Joy:** (see 1 Thessalonians 2:19-20, Daniel 12:3) There is a special reward for those who love the lost and maintain an evangelistic thrust in

their heart. One of the purposes of Christ's coming was to seek and to save that which is lost (see Luke 19:10). Blessed are those who remind the body of Christ to leave the safety of the ninety-nine and seek after the one that has strayed. There is a joy inexpressible and full of glory when the lost come to Christ. Jesus said that the angels have a joyful celebration when just one lost soul comes to Christ (see Luke 15:10).

THERE CAN BE A DISQUALIFICATION

But I discipline my body and bring it into subjection, lest, when I have preached to others, I myself should become disqualified.
— I Corinthians 9:2

Examine yourselves as to whether you are in the faith. Test yourselves. Do you not know yourselves, that Jesus Christ is in you? —unless indeed you are disqualified.
— II Corinthians 13:5

They profess to know God, but in works they deny Him, being abominable, disobedient, and disqualified for every good work.
— Titus 1:16

If there is an approval, then there must also be a disqualification. Many folks these days don't always want to face up to failure and disqualification. They see God as the great enabler in the sky always handing out participation awards. The truth is, He doesn't always praise us. He is not going to say, "well done good and faithful servant" (Matthew 25:21) unless you've been faithful and have done a job well.

There are three different levels of disqualification:

1. Disqualified for advancement or blessing

2. Disqualification for ministry

3. Disqualification for eternal life, or salvation

I'll briefly expound on all three levels:

1. **Disqualification for advancement, or blessing:** If you are not faithful with the little you have, God will not give you more; you have therefore become disqualified for advancement. If you do not tithe and give offerings, you will be disqualified for the promised blessing (see Malachi 3:8-12). The most irritating word in the English language is the two-letter word "IF." It's a lawyer's word. IF you are obedient, then you qualify for the accompanying promise. *"Now it shall come to pass, IF you diligently obey the voice of the Lord your God, to observe carefully all His commandments which I command you today, that the Lord your God will set you high above all nations of the earth. And all these blessings shall come upon you and overtake you, because you obey the voice of the Lord your God"* Deuteronomy 28:1-2.

2. **Disqualification for ministry:** *"For many are called, but few are chosen"* (Matthew 22:14). Some view ministry as an entitlement and not a privilege. Just because you have a call and giftings doesn't mean that God is obligated to use you. I often hear people quote Romans 11:29, *"For the gifts and the callings of God are irrevocable."* The meaning they often imply is that God will never take back His gifts. That is absolutely right! God will not take them back, but He will require an accounting of how we used and developed our gifts. God will not take the gift back, but He doesn't have to use you or your gifts. Many are called, but few have what it takes to see the full development and expansion of their gifts.

A powerful revivalist came to our church when I was a new Christian. Many were healed, decisions were made to follow Jesus and names were added to the Lamb's Book of Life. We found out later that he was having an affair with his secretary and left his wife and children. To top it off, he took the money he raised at our revival meeting that was meant for a mission trip to India and used it to take his secretary to Las Vegas. I asked my wise country pastor how God could use this man so powerfully while he was having an affair. My pastor said, "What makes you think God did those miracles for him? God was not sanctioning this man's sin. God was meeting the needs of His people who had come in faith to receive. God can use a donkey if he wants to." One thing is for sure, what was hidden came to light and the secret sins were eventually revealed. This man's ministry and marriage were destroyed. There was collateral damage as innocent people were hurt by this man's senseless sin. This man became disqualified for any kind of ministry afterward. There may have been some level of restoration if this gifted preacher had repented. When we confess and forsake our sin there is forgiveness, but many times there are still negative consequences in this life.

> *He who covers his sins will not prosper, but whoever confesses and forsakes them will have mercy.*
> *— Proverbs 28:13*

3. **Disqualification for salvation/eternal life:**

Let me start by saying that we serve a loving and faithful God. Our salvation is secure.

- We are kept by the power of God (see Jude 24).
- He is faithful to complete what He has begun in us (see Philippians 1:6).

- No one can snatch us out of the Father's hand (see John 10:28-29).
- Who shall separate us from the love of God (see Romans 8:31-39)?

Although God has extended great grace to you and I, He will never take away your free will. Although no one is able to snatch you from God's love, YOU can walk away any time you want.

- The prodigal son left the Father's love and was dead in sin; "*...for this my son was dead and is alive again; he was lost and is found. And they began to be merry.*" Luke 15:24
- If we do not continue in God's love we risk being cut off. "*Therefore consider the goodness and severity of God: on those who fell, severity; but toward you, goodness, if you continue in His goodness. Otherwise you also will be cut off.*" Romans 11:22
- Why would the Apostle Paul warn us about deception and leaving the faith if it were not possible? "*Now the Spirit expressly says that in latter times some will depart from the faith, giving heed to deceiving spirits and doctrines of demons.*" I Timothy 4:1
- Do not be deceived. A Christian may stumble in sin, but if a Christian persists in a lifestyle of decadence and disobedience they will not inherit the Kingdom of God. That means they will not go to heaven. "*Do you not know that the unrighteous will not inherit the kingdom of God? Do not be deceived. Neither fornicators, nor idolaters, nor adulterers, nor homosexuals, nor sodomites, nor thieves, nor covetous, nor drunkards, nor revilers, nor*

extortioners will inherit the kingdom of God."
I Corinthians 6:9-10

Yes, a Christian can forfeit his salvation. A Christian can be disqualified for eternal life. It's not easy to do. God's love and grace are amazing. He will leave the 99 and go after the one lost. He will sweep the house clean looking for one lost coin. He will put roadblocks up and send divine warnings. He will cause great storms of correction to wake you up from your deception. He never, never, never gives up. If you can count the grains of sand on the seashore, that's how much He thinks about you. So great is His love and keeping power. But we are not robots, and love must be reciprocated. My question is, why would a Christian not stay safely in the hands of such a loving God? Why would anyone want to forfeit on such an epic divine romance?

DO NOT DRAW BACK

Now the just shall live by faith; But if anyone draws back, My soul has no pleasure in him. But we are not of those who draw back to perdition, but of those who believe to the saving of the soul.
— Hebrews 10:38-39

Do not lose heart. Press on to the reward. Blessed is the man who endures. Pass your test. Keep the inner fire burning. People are looking at your life. They need to see you obtain victory. Your advancement and success will encourage so many others.

Take heed to yourself and to the doctrine. Continue in them, for in doing this you will save both yourself and those who hear you.
— I Timothy 4:16

If you continue in the doctrine, you will not only save yourself but you are pulling others with you. Your victory will affect so many other lives.

Let's review this chapter:
- Approval happens after you pass your test
- There is an approval
- God's judgments are in the earth now
- The future judgments of God
- Approval and rewards
- There can be a disqualification
- Do not draw back

Chapter 6

The Mindset of a Winner

GIVE THE EXTRA 2%

*Now these were the men who came to David at Ziklag while he was still a fugitive from Saul the son of Kish; and **they were among the mighty men**, helpers in the war, armed with bows, **using both the right hand and the left** in hurling stones and shooting arrows with the bow. They were of Benjamin, Saul's brethren.*
— I Chronicles 12:1-2

There were warriors in King David's army that distinguished themselves above the rest. They were called the "mighty men" (see 2 Samuel 23:8-39). These were the warrior, rock-star, heroes of the day. Several characteristics elevated these men to mighty man status, but I am focusing on one right now; they gave the extra 2%. Notice that these warriors were proficient with their weapons by using both the right AND left hand. They didn't settle for acceptable standards. They didn't do the bare minimum to pass the weapons proficiency class. They went above and beyond by being able to switch hands for optimum proficiency in battle.

I learned about giving the extra 2% from a preacher. I know there are books and articles written about this, and success gurus apply this principle to inspire excellence. But the first time I heard about it was in a revival meeting. What this old-timer shared has inspired me for years. He shared this principle of excellence using Bible passages like 1 Chronicles 12:1-2 above.

Let's use a hypothetical illustration (although hypothetical, we all know people like this).

There's this guy (completely hypothetical) who was born a gifted, natural athlete. He excelled at every sport. He didn't have to work very hard because things came easily for him. In a rural, small school he was a star, but when he competed at the big college level, sadly, he was average. Because he wasn't used to working hard, he only did what he had to. At the big college level of competition, everyone is a gifted athlete. What separates some to stand out in the pack? Those who give the extra 2%. Just 2% more will cause you to pull ahead. Not just a once in a while 2%, a sustained 2% over a long period of time.

Steve Martin (comedian, actor, musician, and author) was asked what advice he would give to anyone considering a stage career. He said, "Be so good they cannot ignore you." There it is, give that extra 2%.

> *The desire of the lazy man kills him,*
> *for his hands refuse to labor.*
> *— Proverbs 21:25*

Strangely enough, that verse encourages me. There is a goal in my life that has proved elusive. I sensed the Lord witness to my spirit when I read it, "*If you want it, you can have it. But you're going to have to work and sacrifice a little more.*" There it is, give the extra 2% and it's yours. Instead of just dreaming about something, go after it. Work toward it. A little every day is a lot over a year's time. An hour a day is 365 hours a year. How much can you accomplish with 365 hours?

> *Do you see a man who excels in his work? He will stand before kings; He will not stand before unknown men.*
> *— Proverbs 22:29*

BE A LIFELONG LEARNER

> *Wisdom is the principal thing; therefore get wisdom. And in all your getting, get understanding. Exalt her, and she will promote you; she will bring you honor, when you embrace her. She will place on your head an ornament of grace; a crown of glory she will deliver to you.*
> *— Proverbs 4:7-9*

What more needs to be said? The Bible is always encouraging you to learn and grow. There are several very practical ways to improve yourself. The first is to read your Bible. I recommend a "Read the Bible in a Year Plan". A half-hour to an hour a day, reading meditating and journaling will radically change your life and bring you closer to God. Read your Bible for wisdom and greater intimacy with God and you will not be disappointed.

> *This Book of the Law shall not depart from your mouth, but you shall meditate in it day and night, that you may observe to do according to all that is written in it. For then you will make your way prosperous, and then you will have good success.*
> *— Joshua 1:8*

This was the first Bible verse I memorized. Meditation in the Word of God will cause you to make your way prosperous and you will have GOOD success. I was just simple enough to believe it. I didn't need success gurus and infomercials; all I needed was God and His Word.

Some people don't like to be preached at. But everywhere you turn someone is preaching at you; billboard signs, cable TV, fashion magazines, and people are all pushing a lifestyle on you. Why not take God at His word and learn about Him?

Listen to this quote from Jim Rohn (Entrepreneur, millionaire, and motivational speaker):

"Learn to work harder on yourself than you do on your job. If you work hard on your job, you'll make a living, but if you work hard on yourself you'll make a fortune."

Instead of just working to be successful, work on yourself and the person you are becoming. Read books. Get some training. Take a class. Develop your hobby. Find a hobby. Invest in yourself. Determine to be a lifelong learner. Instead of striving for success, seek first the Kingdom of God and let success attract to you (see Matthew 6:33).

> *Now it shall come to pass, if you diligently obey the voice of the Lord your God, to observe carefully all His commandments which I command you today, that the Lord your God will set you high above all nations of the earth.* ***And all these blessings shall come upon you and overtake you,*** *because you obey the voice of the Lord your God.*
> *— Deuteronomy 28:1-2*

As you are growing in your knowledge and obedience, blessings are coming after you! Determine to seek ways to grow and learn. Do not be intimidated. Don't be afraid of criticism. Some people will try and hold you back. They will despise your courage to try new things. They want you to stay in their little safe space of victimhood. You're not a victim, you are victorious in Christ. You are an overcomer.

EVERYTHING WORKS FOR YOUR GOOD

And we know that all things work together for good to those who love God, to those who are the called according to His purpose.
— Romans 8:28

According to this verse, nothing can work against me but only for me. God always has a greater purpose for every trial whether I can comprehend it or not. We walk by faith and not by sight (see 2 Corinthians 5:7). To the unbeliever or atheist, the trials of this life are just random injustices. Probably some culling of the weak to make room for the fit and chosen to survive. Since the universe is running out of energy and will mope down into a slow and excruciating death, nothing makes sense except to be bitter and enraged at being born at all. But to the believer in Christ, God is bringing us to a chosen destiny.

In the book of Genesis, a man named Joseph went through great trials (see Genesis 39-41). Through the things he suffered, his soul came into iron. God molded and toughened Joseph for a great destiny. Although Joseph could not see the purpose of his trials while he was in them, afterward he testified: *"But as for you, you meant evil against me; but God meant it for good, in order to bring it about as it is this day, to save many people alive" (Genesis 50:20).* People say hindsight is always 20/20. Nothing worked against Joseph, but only for him.

> *He sent a man before them — Joseph — who*
> *was sold as a slave.*
> *They hurt his feet with fetters,* **he was laid in irons**
> **(literally – his soul came into iron)**
> **Until the time that his word came to pass,**
> **the word of the LORD tested him.**
> *The king sent and released him;*
> *the ruler of the people let him go free.*
> *He made him lord of his house, and ruler of all his possessions,*
> *To bind his princes at his pleasure, and teach his elders wisdom.*
> *— Psalms 105:17-22*

There was a greater purpose for Joseph's suffering. Joseph was being prepared to lead many to victory. Through his God-given wisdom and the humility gained through suffering, he saved multitudes from pestilence and famine. With the prophetic words of greatness that Joseph received, there was great testing. *"The word of the Lord tested him."* The prophetic dreams Joseph had of his brothers bowing to him tested him. The higher the call, the deeper the character refinement. Now…who would like a prophetic word of greatness after knowing Joseph's story? The word of the Lord will test you, and bring your soul into iron so that God can bring the prophetic word to pass. There is always a humbling, or humility before honor.

> *When they cast you down, and you say, 'Exaltation will come!'*
> *Then He will save* **the humble person.**
> *— Job 22:29*

The fear of the Lord is the instruction of wisdom,
*and **before honor is humility.***
— Proverbs 15:33

TRUST IN THE LORD WHEN YOU DON'T UNDERSTAND

Trust in the Lord with all your heart, and lean not on
your own understanding; In all your ways acknowledge Him,
and He shall direct your paths.
— Proverbs 3:5-6

Funerals can be tough, but I remember one that was extra tough. The young couple were mourning the loss of a three-day-old baby girl. They had been believing for a miracle. The doctor tried convincing them to abort because the fetus had some deformities and the doctor felt the child would not survive outside the womb. Being devout Christians, the couple did not believe in abortion. At prayer meetings, we had laid hands on the Momma's belly and prayed for a creative miracle. The miracle did not come. The couple's worst fears had come upon them.

As I was wrestling with what to say at the funeral, I felt a great peace come over me. The Lord spoke to my spirit in a still small voice, "*The greatest faith is to trust Me when you don't understand.*" I knew immediately that this wisdom came from above. I'm not smart enough to come up with that on my own. The father of the baby never forgot those words I shared; that wisdom helped him through many confusing times. He never gave up on God.

Truth is not limited to my understanding. If I had to completely understand something for it to be true, truth would be very limited. Some things are beyond our ability to comprehend right now. Let's face it, some of the "why" questions will go unanswered this side of heaven. The highest form of faith is to trust Him when you don't understand.

> *For now we see in a mirror, dimly, but then face to face. Now I know in part, but then I shall know just as I also am known.*
> *— I Corinthians 13:12*

There are truths that we accept, and yet don't fully comprehend. For example, The Hypostatic Union: When Jesus was born into this world, He was 100% man (Son of Man) and 100% God (Son of God). That's 200%. That doesn't make sense to the natural mind, and yet it's 100% true. Other examples are that the Bible tells us to die to self and find life; give and you will have more than enough; you must be born again to have eternal life; and, if you look to the needs of others you will have fulfillment. The Kingdom of God seems like an upside-down kingdom.

I can understand theologically that because sin and death are in the world, children sometimes die. But that doesn't ease the pain of loss. Nor the enraged sense of injustice we may feel. The only way to get through these types of personal crises and not grow bitter is to trust God when we don't understand. I have seen people marooned on a deserted island of grief and loss for years until they decided to light a signal fire and rejoin civilization. At some point, we must move forward. The living need us. God has things for us to do. If you are still breathing, it's because you still have a great purpose.

> *"For I know the plans I have for you," says the Lord.*
> *"They are plans for good and not for disaster,*
> *to give you a future and a hope."*
> *— Jeremiah 29:11 NLT*

For we are God's masterpiece. He has created us anew in Christ Jesus, so we can do the good things he planned for us long ago.
— Ephesians 2:10

NEVER GIVE UP

*Blessed is the man who **endures temptation**; for when he has been approved, he will receive the crown of life which the Lord has promised to those who love Him.*
— James 1:12 NKJV

*Blessed (happy, to be envied) is the man who is **patient under trial** and stands up under temptation, for when he has stood the test and been approved, he will receive [the victor's] crown of life which God has promised to those who love Him.*
— James 1:12 AMP

As we look at James 1:12, notice the phrase "patient under trial," or "Blessed is the man who endures." Endurance, patience, and perseverance are major qualities in the success of any endeavor. I would say that most, if not all, of the accomplishments in my life were because of sheer dogged perseverance. What I lacked in talent, I made up for by just plain sticking with it. What has always amazed me is when someone has been gifted with an amazing aptitude but has no perseverance. When the most minuscule of challenges come their way, they give up and quit. It doesn't matter how gifted a person is, sooner or later guts and determination will be required.

When I was a child, my mother would read books to me before bed. I had a favorite book that I insisted we read almost every night, "The Little Engine That Could." In the story, a trainload of toys and treats were abandoned on the side of the tracks because the engine that was supposed to take them to the children on the other side of the mountain had broken down. Along came this smaller, happy-go-lucky engine. The toys and play animals beg the little engine to take them to the other side of the mountain because there were children over there waiting for them. The little engine explains that he is just used for moving cars around in the train yard and had never been used to pull a whole train before. After a little more persuasion, the little engine hooks up to the front of the broken down train and starts slowly chugging along.

The little engine began speaking this steady rhythm of positive affirmation through his smokestack: "I think I can, I think I can, I think I can...." Against all odds, and overcoming many obstacles, the little engine made the journey. I was completely enamored by the power of persistence. An impartation got into me from that book, and an unshakable idea entered my head, "If a person persisted long enough and worked hard enough, almost anything can be accomplished."

After I became a Christian, I discovered that the power of perseverance must be aimed at the right goals and for the right things. A person can be stubborn and bull-headed in a direction that God has not blessed, which can cause many heartaches. Make sure you are submitting your plans, purposes, and pursuits to the Lord. Even when God gives you the green light, you will still be required to persevere for many things.

> *And we desire that each one of you show the same diligence to the full assurance of hope until the end, that you do*

> *not become sluggish, but imitate those who through faith*
> *and patience inherit the promises.*
> *— Hebrews 6:11-12*

"Faith and Patience" are the power twins of the Bible. If we are to endure and overcome trials, setbacks, and obstacles, we must persevere. When a promise does not manifest quickly, don't assume that it's not God's will. Just because a promise is given doesn't mean that God will do it all. God promised the land of Canaan to Abraham and his children, but they still had to partner with God and conquer the land. God worked with them but there was still a work of faith that needed to be done. There is the perseverance of prayer. There is the faithfulness in small steps. Faith without works is dead, and faith must be coupled with patience for promises to be realized. When you are willing to wait in faith forever, you may not need to wait that long. The victory could be right around the next bend in the road. Never give up!

> *And let us not grow weary while doing good, for in due season*
> *we shall reap if we do not lose heart.*
> *— Galatians 6:9*

JESUS ALWAYS LEADS US TO VICTORY

> *Now thanks be to God who **always leads us in triumph in Christ**,*
> *and through us diffuses the fragrance of His knowledge*
> *in every place.*
> *— 2 Corinthians 2:14*

> *But thanks be to God, who gives us the victory through*
> *our Lord Jesus Christ.*
> *— 1 Corinthians 15:57*

God is not a man that He should lie; it's impossible for Him to lie. These verses state that God ALWAYS leads us to triumph in Christ. Somehow there is a victory to be achieved and somehow God can get glory out of any situation. We just have to follow His lead. Where He leads we will follow. Even when we are the cause of our troubles, if we come to Him with a broken and contrite heart, God will bring some sort of restoration. Don't let self-pity and guilt cloud your ability to see the way of escape.

> No temptation has overtaken you except such as is common to man; but God is faithful, who will not allow you to be tempted beyond what you are able, but with the temptation will also make the way of escape, that you may be able to bear it.
> — 1 Corinthians 10:13

The word for temptation here can also be a trial. The promise here is that God will not allow the trials of this world to overwhelm you. There is nothing you can't handle with Him at your side. There is a way through whatever this evil age can throw at you. The Lord is the strength of my life (see Psalm 27:1). He can infuse you and me with spiritual might and strength in the inner man to overcome any obstacle (see Ephesians 3:16).

- Strength can be imparted by the Holy Spirit
  – Ephesians 3:16
- Strength can be imparted through the Word of God
  – Proverbs 4:20-22
- Strength can be imparted by the ministry of angels
  – Luke 22:43, Hebrews 1:14
- Strength can be imparted by the prayers of the saints
  – Ephesians 6:18, Philippians 1:19

Nothing can work against me but only for me (see Romans 8:28). Somehow God can turn what seems to be a defeat into a victory. All things work together for my good. God has a special grace for every situation. We have to learn to receive the grace, to grab hold of it, and allow that grace to carry us (see 2 Corinthians 12:9).

When you are going through a trial, don't hide out and separate yourself from church fellowship. Go to every prayer meeting you can. Go to every worship service you can. This is when you need to be surrounded by good Christian people who will constantly pray with you and encourage you. The worst thing you can do is isolate yourself. You have nothing to be ashamed of. There's not a person alive who has gone through this life unscathed by various trials. *"Yet man is born to trouble, as the sparks fly upward" (Job 5:7).* It's important to receive grace and mercy from others. It's also important to give grace and mercy to those going through a trial. Don't be Job's friends who pointed out all his sins as he was going through the greatest trial of his life. Sow mercy towards your future. There will come an evil day when you will need to make a withdrawal of grace and mercy (see Ephesians 6:13).

APPROVAL COMES WHEN WE BLEND TRUTH WITH MERCY

For he who serves Christ in these things is acceptable to God and approved by men.
— Romans 14:18

The approval that comes from God is always more important than the approval of men. When we are in God's favor, can't He open doors that were once closed to us? Can't the all sovereign Lord of the universe cause favor with judges, magistrates, and governors? Men of position are subject to Him, and He can turn the King's heart wherever He wishes.

> *The king's heart is in the hand of the Lord, Like the rivers of water; He turns it wherever He wishes.*
> *— Proverbs 21:1*

You also will need the approval of men at times. As a senior pastor, I receive recommendation forms that must be turned in for folks to be approved and accepted into different schools and to serve in different ministries. I mostly give very favorable reports. Once I was tempted to give a favorable recommendation just to get relief from an underwhelming person in the church. If he/she was shipped out to this ministry halfway across the country, many of my problems would have been over. (Hey, I'm just being honest.) I couldn't do it though; I would have felt too guilty sending all those woes to a sincere ministry.

To be a person who receives favor and approval from God and man, you must also learn to blend truth with mercy and grace. Some are weak in holding people to the truth, while others are weak in giving grace.

> *Let not mercy and truth forsake you; bind them around your neck, write them on the tablet of your heart, and so find favor and high esteem in the sight of God and man.*
> *— Proverbs 3:3-4*

It is often said that the truth hurts. The truth can be ice cold and unforgiving. The truth can also be so unbearable that in some cases it would be better not to know it. Some use the truth as a club to beat down others and claim, "I only speak the truth." In the Bible, you see truth coupled with love, mercy, and grace.

> *All the paths of the LORD are mercy and truth.*
> *— Psalms 25:10a*

> *Do not withhold Your tender mercies from me, O LORD; let Your loving kindness and Your truth continually preserve me.*
> *— Psalms 40:11*

> *Mercy and truth have met together; righteousness and peace have kissed.*
> *— Psalms 85:10*

> *For the law was given through Moses, but grace and truth came through Jesus Christ.*
> *— John 1:17*

> *But, speaking the truth in love, may grow up in all things into Him who is the head — Christ —*
> *— Ephesians 4:15*

Unless truth is tempered with love and grace, its transforming power will be limited. Some folks become imbalanced and swing way over to the truth side, while others want to swing way over on the grace side. (The truth side being too harsh and the grace side is too enabling.) There must be a successful blend of the two for the release of a new level of favor on your life; favor from God and man. We must learn to rightly divide the Word of God. When we learn the true character of God and work to always bring restoration, the Holy Spirit unveils profound truth.

> *Be diligent to present yourself **approved** to God,*
> *a worker who does not need to be ashamed,*
> *rightly dividing the Word of truth.*
> *— 2 Timothy 2:15*

We are to be approved by God and have great favor with men. We must look to the reward and persevere. We must access God's inexhaustible grace and strength, and we must rightly divide the Word of truth. If you always maintain the attitude of restoration and not retaliation, and if you are always seeking peace, as much as lies in you, the God of peace will be with you and you will be approved.

Let's review the mindsets you must have to overcome:

- Give the extra 2%
- Be a lifelong learner/keep developing yourself
- Everything will work for your good/Trust God and be obedient
- Trust in the Lord when you don't understand
- Never give up/Faith and patience inherit the promises
- Jesus will always lead you to victory/Be willing to follow
- Approval comes when we blend truth with mercy

Chapter 7

The Storms of Life

Then they cry out to the LORD in their trouble,
And He brings them out of their distresses.
He calms the storm,
So that its waves are still.
Then they are glad because they are quiet;
So He guides them to their desired haven.
— Psalm 107:28-30

I have never been in a storm at sea. I have been on Lake Michigan when the waves were hammering and unrelenting. Mariners tell me that the waves on the Great Lakes are different than the ocean. On the Great Lakes, they are smaller, closer together and choppier. On the ocean, they pitch like rolling high hills, deep canyons and then huge mountainous peaks. Even the saltiest of sailors never stop being in awe of the power and vastness of the ocean. Sometimes peaceful in a meditative solitude, and other times enraged; foaming up shards of glassy waves, and spitting out effervescent white caps of spray. As if the waves were shaking a fist at God, they slam down defiantly on the rocky shores, recklessly trying to prevail over all boundaries that God has set for it.

> *"Do you not fear Me?" says the LORD.*
> *"Will you not tremble at My presence,*
> *Who have placed the sand as the bound of the sea,*
> *By a perpetual decree, that it cannot pass beyond it?*
> *And though its waves toss to and fro,*
> *Yet they cannot prevail;*
> *Though they roar, yet they cannot pass over it."*
> *— Jeremiah 5:22*

> *When I said,*
> *"This far you may come, but no farther,*
> *And here your proud waves must stop!"*
> *— Job 38:11*

God sets boundaries against the crashing sea, so it is with the tempests of life. Their proud and angry waves can go thus far, and no more. For the Christian, there are responses and defenses against these storms. Our God can do exceedingly, abundantly, above all that the storms of life can bring. When the enemy comes in like a flood, the Spirit of the Lord will lift up a standard against him (see Isaiah 59:19). God has not left us orphaned and at the mercy of the billowing surf. God will bring peace to the storm. He knows how to bring you to your desired haven.

As we progress in our spiritual journey, we will be assaulted by three different types of storms: the storm of correction, the storm of opposition, and random storms of life. Life is full of unplanned obstacles and setbacks. Having discernment into these different types of storms, and how to appropriately respond to them, will help you advance. The unbeliever does not possess this wisdom. As a Christian, you have a divine perspective that will give you peace, and empower you to face life's gales with courage and tenacity.

STORMS OF CORRECTION

*But the LORD sent out a great wind on the sea,
and there was a mighty tempest on the sea,
so that the ship was about to be broken up.
— Jonah 1:4
(Please read Jonah, chapter one)*

The first storm of life that we want to discuss is the storm of correction. This type of storm is taught clearly in the book of Jonah. I have never questioned the story of Jonah. It wasn't until Bible College that I became aware that many scholars thought it to be a Jewish myth. How could anyone who believes that the Bible is the inspired Word of God EVER conclude that the book of Jonah was a myth?!? If you try to take the supernatural and miraculous out of the Bible, you're not left with much. You're left with a leather cover, a concordance, and some maps. If a person has trouble with the miraculous nature of the Bible, then they will have serious trouble with the very first verse. *"In the beginning, God created the heavens and the earth. Genesis 1:1.*

My grandmother was one of those who wrestled with the fantastic stories of the Bible. Once when I visited her, she was excited to announce that scholars had found where the Children of Israel had crossed the Red Sea. She explained how the place that they crossed had only six inches of water. She then smugly glared at me waiting for a response. She knew I never would have agreed to any attempt to rationally explain away the miracles of the Bible.

I said, "Grandma, it's a miracle!"

"How do you figure?"

"That God could drown the whole Egyptian army in SIX inches of water! Think of it?!"

"Oh, you make me so mad!" Grandma responded.

Thus, the argument was concluded. Moral of the story: It's impossible to take the miraculous out of the Bible and still have the Bible make sense.

Jonah's storm came because he was in rebellion against God. You can have understanding and patience with someone who is ignorant of God's will and is in confusion. Not the case with Jonah. He had clearly heard the voice of God that he was to warn the Ninevites about God's coming judgment. He was a seasoned prophet who knew the Lord. Because of his prejudice and hatred for the Assyrian people, Jonah would rather see them judged and wiped out than to have them find favor with God. The Assyrians were a powerful and cruel enemy to his people, and Nineveh was their capital city. In Jonah's mind, it was hard to grasp why God would give them a chance to repent. He should just exterminate them and be done with it. They deserved judgment, not a chance to repent and find mercy.

In Jonah's attempt to run from the call of God, he found a seafaring vessel headed toward Tarshish, which was almost the exact opposite direction of God's calling to warn the Ninevites. When the storm was in full bloom, and the mariners were calling on their gods for mercy, Jonah was asleep in the lowest part of the ship. This was a sleep of apathy. He didn't care about himself, the mariners, or the city of Nineveh. Disobedience doesn't take place in a void. When we sin, it affects those around us, and the more authority and responsibility we carry, the greater the extent of our influence. The sins of bitterness and unforgiveness are not only destructive to us but also to the people around us. I've heard it said that refusing to forgive is like drinking poison and hoping your enemy dies. The infectious nature of bitterness is well stated in the following verse:

> *Looking carefully lest anyone fall short of the grace of God;*
> *lest any root of bitterness springing up cause trouble,*
> *and by this many become defiled.*
> *— Hebrews 12:15*

What can we learn about the character of God in the story of Jonah? I have often heard from Bible teachers that the Old Testament portrays a God of judgment, while the New Testament portrays a God of grace. I don't see it that way. I see a God of tremendous patience, mercy and grace in the Old Testament. I also see some Old Testament-style judgment in the book of Acts and Revelation. I see a consistency in the way God responds to the level of revelation a person or nation has received. The ways of God are consistent. If we persist in sin we go into further judgment. If we show contrition and repent, there is mercy and restoration. *"For I am the Lord, I do not change" (see Malachi 3:6a).* Although God changed His mind and did not destroy Nineveh, He did not change His ways and character. When we respond to His correction and warnings, He is faithful to relent.

- We see that God rises early and sends His messengers. He is faithful to never leave Himself without a witness (see 2 Chronicles 36:15-16).
- God always warns before he brings retribution on sin.

- If we will not listen to God's inner witness, He will use people and/or circumstances to correct us. With Jonah it was the storm and the mariners; with Nineveh it was Jonah (see 1 Corinthians 11:31-32).
- If we show sincere sorrow for sin and change our ways, then God changes His disposition towards us and brings blessing instead of judgment (see 1 John 1:9).

When a storm of correction comes to your life, it will come in two forms:

First, there is a law woven into the fabric of the universe called the law of seedtime and harvest, or sowing and reaping.

While the earth remains, seedtime and harvest, cold and heat, winter and summer, and day and night shall not cease.
— Genesis 8:22

Do not be deceived, God is not mocked; for whatever a man sows, that he will also reap.
— Galatians 6:7

Not every storm is a direct judgment from God. Some storms we bring on ourselves. Sin has consequences and carries its own judgment. My mother used to say, "Give somebody enough rope and they'll hang themselves." In other words, don't worry about somebody getting away with something. Eventually, their sin will find them out (see Numbers 32:23). The wages of sin is death, and the principle of death works ruination when we offend the righteousness of God.

Something I discovered about the law of sowing and reaping is that God holds the control switch on how much we reap. He can choose to suspend and hold back a nasty harvest.

Think about it, if we all reaped what we deserve, we would all go to hell, but the total harvest from our sin is canceled in Christ. God can allow just enough reaping in this life to work its discipline. When we cry out to Him, confess our sin and turn from our wicked ways, then He can choose to cancel out our harvest. When I was a young man and not serving the Lord, I would sow my wild oats and pray for a crop failure.

God not only suspends the reaping of a bad harvest, but He also sometimes enhances a harvest, to become super fruitful. He can increase the fruits of our righteousness (see 2 Corinthians 9:10). Observe how the Lord brought a supernatural harvest to Isaac in the time of famine.

> *Then Isaac sowed in that land, and reaped in the same year a hundredfold; and the LORD blessed him. The man began to prosper, and continued prospering until he became very prosperous; for he had possessions of flocks and possessions of herds and a great number of servants. So the Philistines envied him.*
> *— Genesis 26:12-14*

The **second** form of correction is direct judgment. Direct judgment from God is a last-ditch effort to turn us. God doesn't arbitrarily bring destruction to people or nations. He doesn't wake up in a bad mood and start chucking lightning bolts at unsuspecting sinners. Phases of correction look something like this:

- Conviction of conscience, an inner witness of wrong – Romans 9:1.
- God will send His word through prophets, pastors and mature believers – 2 Chronicles 36:16.

- God allows some reaping from our stubbornness – Galatians 6:7.
- God intervenes directly with a full exposure of sin (see Proverbs 5:14). Although God can allow us to reap for our sins, or remove His covering of protection so the devil can bring destruction, He doesn't always use the devil to judge. His act of just vengeance can be a holy thing – Leviticus 10:1-3, Acts 5:1-11, Acts 12:20-24, Proverbs 6:15.

Another thing my mother used to say is, "If you get yourself in a hole, stop digging." If you find yourself in a storm of correction, why continue to destruction? Confess and turn from what you know is wrong. Find help from accountability groups (12 step programs). If you sincerely want to turn your course, cry out to the Lord. He specializes in saving sinners.

We see something else happening in this first chapter of Jonah. The mariners became caught up in Jonah's storm of correction. They had done nothing but were about to be collateral damage in the conflict between Jonah and the Almighty.

> *And he said to them, "Pick me up and throw me into the sea; then the sea will become calm for you. For I know that this great tempest is because of me." Nevertheless the men rowed hard to return to land, but they could not, for the sea continued to grow more tempestuous against them.*
> *— Jonah 1:12-13*

The mariners did not want to do the hard thing and throw Jonah into the tempestuous sea. In their attempt to be merciful they became unwitting accomplices in his rebellion.

They became enablers, and in their misplaced mercy were shielding Jonah from God's discipline.

There are times when we are caught in the crossfire of warfare. A bad place to be is standing right between God and a person He is correcting. This is where the discernment of the Holy Spirit comes in. If you are in a storm aimed at someone else, release them to God. Stop helping them in their rebellion. The storm got to the point where the mariners had to throw Jonah overboard. If they had done nothing, the storm would have destroyed them.

A distraught married couple met me at my office. They had decided to help a seventeen-year-old boy by letting him live in their home. At that time they had three children of their own living at home, the oldest was in the ninth grade. To live in their home, they established some rules for the seventeen-year-old by which he was to follow. This young man consistently broke those rules and stayed out all night drinking and disregarding all restraints. The husband of the home wanted to follow through with the agreement they had originally established, that if he broke those rules, he would no longer be able to live there. The wife wanted to show mercy and keep giving him chances. As we prayed, God showed me the story of Jonah. The husband and wife were the mariners, their home was the ship tossed by the waves. They wanted to show mercy and row to land but the storm just kept getting worse. I told them they had to throw the young man overboard or their household would be destroyed. After some tears on the wife's part, I asked if she felt that I was hearing from God. She said yes, my advice was from the Lord. The couple agreed to take the young man to his dad's house.

When they arrived at their home, the wife said that she needed to be the one to drop him off at his dad's home. On the way, she had a change of heart and came back home with the young man. The husband was furious. He told his wife that either he (the young man) leaves or they can both leave. Well, they both left and this led to the destruction of their household. Divorce ensued with all of the heartaches.

Sometimes our charity can be toxic. Once I was taking a couple of boxes of groceries to a needy couple and while I was driving to their home the Holy Spirit spoke to me, "Why are you giving them steaks when I have them on corn husks?" I was blown away. It never occurred to me that I might be standing in the way of God's righteous discipline. Please don't misinterpret me here, I am not saying that all charity is wrong. Nor am I creating a convenient excuse to absent ourselves from helping others. This was a unique circumstance. If I would have helped this couple, I would have been caught up in their storm of correction.

One day I picked up the church phone when my administrative assistant wasn't there. The girl on the other end seemed sweet and sincere. She asked if the church could pay her rent. She had one child and she was living with her boyfriend. I asked if she could go home and live with her parents. She said she couldn't because her parents didn't like her boyfriend, nor did they agree with her living with him. I said, "Think about what you are asking the church to do. You are asking us to pay for you to live with your boyfriend out of wedlock and be in rebellion against your good folks." I did suggest to her an organization from which she could get food for her and her baby. I never heard from her again. Although

I felt bad for her circumstance and that she was dragging a young child through it all, I did not want the church to be caught up in her storm of correction.

If you are going through a storm of correction, turn from what you know is wrong. Confess your sin to God and He will help you out of all the storm damage around you. If you are caught up in the crossfire of someone else's correction, pray for wisdom. God will show you what to do to save yourself and the person and/or persons you are shielding from God's loving correction (see James 1:5).

He who covers his sins will not prosper,
But whoever confesses and forsakes them will have mercy.
— Proverbs 28:13

If we confess our sins, He is faithful and just to forgive us our sins and to cleanse us from all unrighteousness.
— 1 John 1:9

STORMS OF OPPOSITION

On the same day, when evening had come, He said to them, "Let us cross over to the other side." Now when they had left the multitude, they took Him along in the boat as He was. And other little boats were also with Him. And a great windstorm arose, and the waves beat into the boat, so that it was already filling. But He was in the stern, asleep on a pillow. And they awoke Him and said to Him, "Teacher, do You not care that we are perishing?" Then He arose and rebuked the wind, and said to the sea, "Peace, be still!" And the wind ceased and there was a great calm. But He said to them, "Why are you so fearful? How is it that you have no faith?" And they feared exceedingly,

> *and said to one another, "Who can this be, that even the wind and the sea obey Him!"*
> — Mark 4:35-41

The ministry team had a clear word from Christ, "Let us cross over to the other side." They were not in rebellion or disobedient to His command, and yet in doing what they were told to do, a deadly storm rose up and tried to wipe them out. We will face opposition as we advance the Gospel and the Kingdom of God. Satan and his minions are not just going to lie down and let you steamroll all over them. *As we invade and raid hell to populate heaven, there will be spiritual warfare.*

Our response to a storm of correction is to repent; our response to a storm of opposition is to fight! Many don't know the difference. Like the disciples in this story, they are at the mercy of the tempest. Or worse, they just take it and blame God. We sometimes rebuke storms of correction and put up with storms of opposition. What we need is wisdom and discernment to not only know the difference but to know how to respond appropriately.

> *If any of you lacks wisdom, let him ask of God, who gives to all liberally and without reproach, and it will be given to him.*
> — James 1:5

Jesus rebuked the storm of opposition and there was a great calm. That is not the part of the story that amazes me; it's when Jesus chided His disciples and said, "Why are you so fearful? How is it that you have no faith?" What was He expecting out of them? What did He want them to do?

Let's look at some possibilities:

A. He wanted them to just take it and endure the storm

because they should have known that somehow they would make it, even though the boat was taking on water and sinking.

B. He expected them to rise up and rebuke the storm. If the mission was to get to the other side, then they needed to take authority over any demonic opposition that would manifest against them.

Most people pick option A. After all, only God can speak to a storm; we shouldn't be ordering around storms. Then the falsely humble religionist says, "What kind of pride are you in? You can't start taking authority and declaring things. Do you think you're God?"

Jesus was training His disciples to use the spiritual authority that was delegated to them. He knew they would be facing some great opposition and would need to be trained in how to do effective spiritual warfare. In all training, there are tests to see how you will implement what you have been taught. Do you know who you are as a child of God? Do you know your authority in Christ? I think that if we have a true revelation of the greatness of His power toward us who believe, it would frighten us. Jesus and the Word of God instruct us that there is spiritual authority and power in our words and declarations.

> *For assuredly, I say to you, whoever says to this mountain, 'Be removed and be cast into the sea,' and does not doubt in his heart, but believes that those things he says will be done, he will have whatever he says. Therefore I say to you, whatever things you ask when you pray, believe that you receive them, and you will have them.*
> — *Mark 11:23-24*

> *You will also declare a thing,*
> *And it will be established for you;*
> *So light will shine on your ways.*
> *— Job 22:28*

> *Death and life are in the power of the tongue,*
> *And those who love it will eat its fruit.*
> *— Proverbs 18:21*

The Bible is very clear that our words have power. When God tells you to declare over a situation, you are not bringing your own words to bear on the problem. You are speaking in the Name of Christ. You are declaring over something that Jesus Himself would declare. This is called a prophetic declaration.

The prophet Ezekiel was told by God to prophesy over an army of dry bones. *"Prophesy to these dry bones, and say to them, 'O dry bones, hear the word of the Lord!'" (Ezekiel 37:4).* God wants us to prophesy over some things. It's not prideful to obey God when He tells you to prophesy over something. Perhaps God is waiting on you to take authority over the storm? You are not at the mercy of any demonic attack. We don't have to be fearful disciples cowering underneath the storm. Our faith is not in the fearful storm, our faith is in God Almighty. He has not given us a spirit of fear, but of power, love and a sound mind (see 2 Timothy 1:7)! Jesus has given us authority and power over devils; they are subject to us in His name.

> *Behold, I give you the authority to trample on serpents*
> *and scorpions, and over all the power of the enemy,*
> *and nothing shall by any means hurt you. Nevertheless*
> *do not rejoice in this, that the spirits are subject to you,*
> *but rather rejoice because your names are written in heaven.*
> *— Luke 10:19-20*

Serpents and scorpions are emblems of evil spirits, and you have been given authority over them. Don't get a big head about it, just be thankful that your name is written in the Book of Life.

The test in the storm of opposition is whether or not you are going to overcome it. You must learn to engage the enemy in combat. The Holy Spirit has tactical wisdom for every situation. When Joshua was leading the nation of Israel in conquest of the land of Canaan, God gave him strategies for every battle. The strategy that was used on the city of Jericho was never employed again. Each type of opposition causes you to seek God for the best way to adapt and overcome. Here are some different ways to engage the enemy. This in no way is exhaustive, these are the basics:

- **Prayer and fasting** (see Matthew 17:21, Esther 4:16): This is the nuke of spiritual warfare. In the book of Esther, Haman tried to annihilate the entire Jewish race. When the Haman spirit comes to annihilate you, your ministry and revival, prayer and fasting is the only way to deliver a knockout blow.
- **Renewing your mind** (see Romans 12:2, John 8:32, 2 Corinthians 10:3-5): The truth of God's Word will set you free. Renewing your mind and getting God's perspective on things will always bring hope and victory. A Christian with a mind renewed on the promises of God, and who knows who he is in Christ, is a dangerous person to the Kingdom of darkness. In Ephesians chapter six, putting on the armor of God is a Christian equipped and properly trained in the use of the Sword of the Spirit, which is the Word of God.
- **Obedience to God** (see James 4:7): Simply obeying

God drives opposition away. Resisting the devil is as simple as obeying God. When the Holy Spirit gives you strategies to implement, you must walk them out. You must walk out obedience to the Word of God. You must walk out what He has shown us in prayer and fasting. Sometimes God does it all, other times there must be a cooperation on your part; an act of obedience.

- **Prophetic declaration** (see Proverbs 18:21): We must declare in the Name of Jesus what God shows us in His Word. We must come into agreement with God and say what He is saying. Jesus rebuked the winds and waves of opposition. He is our example, as He is, so are we in this world (see 1 John 4:17). Stand up and take your authority.

You have been drafted into a war. There will be spiritual opposition. Pick up your sword and attack. God has not left you helpless. He will fight with you, but you must rise up against opposition. He is not in the business of raising up weak, emaciated believers. He is raising up spiritual warriors who are a dread to the powers of darkness. God is training us to plunder the treasuries of hell, rescue souls and rout principalities and powers, making an open show of them. We are sons and daughters of the King of Kings, this is our legacy, and all the saints have this honor (see Psalms 149:6-9).

THE STORMS OF LIFE

> *Therefore whoever hears these sayings of Mine, and does them, I will liken him to a wise man who built his house on the rock: and the **rain descended, the floods came, and the winds blew and beat on that house;** and it did not fall, for it was founded on the rock.*

The Storms of Life

> *"But everyone who hears these sayings of Mine, and does not do them, will be like a foolish man who built his house on the sand: and the **rain descended, the floods came, and the winds blew and beat on that house**; and it fell. And great was its fall.*
> — *Matthew 7:24-27*

If you notice in the above passage, no one is exempt from the storms of life. The winds blow and the storms rage against all, whether you build your house on the rock or sand. The difference is that the one who heeded the words of Christ survived the onslaught of enraged winds and rain.

This storm represents the random uncertainties in a fallen world. If I have to go through the valley of the shadow of death, and if I have to be assaulted by a dark sinful world, I will do so with God. A thousand may fall at my side, and ten thousand at my left, but it shall not come near me (see Psalms 91). And if I do fall, even if I fall seven times, God is able to raise me up again (see Proverbs 24:16). He is able to sustain me; He is able to make me stand (Romans 14:4).

Some friends of mine had fallen into some financial trouble. They were several months behind on their payments for their resort property. Aside from a miracle from God, they saw no way out of this predicament. There was no refinancing available and they were about to be evicted. We prayed fervently with these precious saints about this crisis. It was hard to ascertain how they had found themselves in this fix, but blame-shifting was not going to solve the problem. A great tempestuous storm had hit them.

During prayer one night, God spoke to my friend this verse: Acts 27:22 - *"And now I urge you to take heart, for there will be no loss of life among you, but only of the ship."* I asked him if he could tell me what God was speaking to him through this verse. He explained that although they were going to lose the resort, their family would survive and they would be okay. They ended up losing their property but obtained an affordable home without the unbearable stress of huge payments. God did great things for them and held their family together through this crisis. In fact, they found themselves in a better situation than before the financial storm arose. Those who build their house upon the rock will stand.

The world is watching. People want hope; when they observe you going through a storm, they want to know if your faith helps. The greatest witness that you can have is to persevere through a raging blizzard. When I was a young Christian, I used to think that if I was perfect enough and never had any troubles, everyone I knew would want to become a Christian. Well, guess what? I could never be perfect enough or escape the challenges of life. I began to discover that what folks wanted was NOT to see some self-righteous nerd; what they wanted was hope. If faith in Christ caused me to overcome, then maybe it could work for them. *"The name of the Lord is a strong tower; the righteous run to it and are safe"* (Proverbs 18:10).

When we are hit with a storm of correction, the proper response is to turn from what we know is wrong and God will deliver us and bring restoration.

When we are attacked with a storm of opposition, we are being put to the test. We need to use the spiritual weapons and strategy that God reveals and fight it through to victory.

As we build our life on the sayings of Christ and the full council of God's Word, we are in preparation for the random storms of life. We can weather the storms of life; the Lord is able to make us stand.

*Are you going to please people
and give in to their demands,
or are you going to please God?*

Chapter 8

Loving the Praise of Men

For I am not ashamed of the gospel of Christ, for it is the
power of God to salvation for everyone who believes,
for the Jew first and also for the Greek.
— Romans 1:16

But as we have been approved by God to be entrusted
*with the gospel, even so we speak, **not as pleasing men,***
but God who tests our hearts.
— I Thessalonians 2:4

I am a recovering people pleaser. I would like to create a 12-step support group called "People Pleasers Anonymous." Instead of striving to have "peace at all cost", our new slogan would be, "You can't please everyone." When our meetings come to a close, we will confess in unison "NO MORE MISTER NICE GUY!" We will train ourselves NOT to laugh at dumb jokes just to be polite to idiots. We will NEVER apologize unless we have actually done something wrong. We will practice looking each other in the eye and say "NO" with conviction. And, we will avoid the need to constantly fish for compliments.

Before I became a Christian, I lived for acceptance and positive affirmation. I was very affable and had many friends.

I prided myself at being the life of the party. Five years before I gave my life to Christ I was presented with the gospel, but I rejected it because I knew it would cost me my friends. I loved the acceptance of my friends more than the acceptance of God. I thought that giving my life to Christ meant I had to resign myself to a lonely, boring life. Even though Jesus said, "*I came that they may have life, and that they may have it more abundantly*" *(John 10:10b)*, I couldn't grasp with my puny brain how I could possibly have fun without attending a drunken beer bash.

One night after an excessive celebration, I was in a terrible car accident. I broke my jaw in seven places and had to suck my food through a straw for a month. This was one of those ah-ha times I chose to reconsider my life and realized that God needed to be more important than my friends. After giving my life to Christ, what I feared came upon me. No one wanted to spend time with a Jesus freak who no longer was a drunken fool. I would confess to myself daily that, "I am not ashamed of the gospel of Christ." I bore the full brunt of rejection from several sources and knew that if I was going to be successful in following Jesus, I had to be broken of my fear of man. Finally, I cried out to the Lord and He led me to this scripture verse and made me a promise:

> *Then Peter began to say to Him, "See, we have left all and followed You." So Jesus answered and said, "Assuredly, I say to you, there is no one who has left house or brothers or sisters or father or mother or wife or children or lands, for My sake and the gospel's, who shall not receive a hundredfold now in this time — houses and*

> *brothers and sisters and mothers and children and lands, with*
> *persecutions — and in the age to come, eternal life.*
> *— Mark 10:28-30*

After reading these verses I knew what God was saying to me. He was encouraging me that if I stayed persistent in my commitment to serve Christ, I would reap a harvest of friends. It's impossible for God to lie; if He promises that you will receive a hundredfold in this life, He means it. The hundredfold return speaks not just of quantity, but quality. Friendships based on the depth of your faith in Christ are much richer then friendships based on beer parties. Slowly I began to make friends in the body of Christ until now I abound with friends all over the nation and some in different parts of the globe.

I knew I had to break free from needing the praises of people. I knew I had to pass my test. One of the hardest things for me to understand was that not everyone was going to like me. I mean, why would you not like me? I'm not being conceited; I have always considered myself very jovial and easy going. And now that I had given my life to Christ, I just alienated myself from a whole segment of the population. In following Christ, you will inevitably be faced with THE choice: Am I going to please people and give in to their demands, or am I going to please God? The sooner you learn to stand on your own, rooted and grounded in the love of God, the better you will be. The alternative is to be a milk toast, wishy washy, spineless jellyfish, pushed around and tossed to and fro by every wind of sentiment. I've heard it said that if you stand for nothing, you'll fall for anything. If you are to advance and become a leader, you must develop the moral courage to stand alone against opposition.

> *Am I now trying to win the approval of men, or of God?*
> *Or am I trying to please men? If I were still trying to please men,*
> *I would not be a servant of Christ.*
> — Galatians 1:10 NIV

If you become a follower of Jesus, you WILL be tested on this issue. It will be to your benefit to overcome a need for constant approval. I was working as a cook in a restaurant and a co-worker came to me very excited about something great that was happening in his life. I spontaneously wanted to say, "Praise the Lord!" but I caught myself, realizing that I was not in church. I immediately felt conviction from the Holy Spirit, "Why didn't you say 'Praise the Lord?'" I didn't have a good answer. Why should I be one way in church and another way at work? From that day forward I decided that if something deserved a hardy, "Praise the Lord!" I would proclaim it freely. I have to always remind myself, "I am not ashamed of the Gospel of Christ, for it is the power of God to salvation for everyone who believes!"

When you make a wholehearted decision to serve Christ, the dynamics of all your relationships will change. Some people will choose not to accept you as a follower of Christ. Some may even turn on you and persecute you, in not so subtle ways. The reality is that whether you serve Christ or not, there will always be those who will not like you. It's much easier to handle rejection when you have the unconditional acceptance of God. Determine to serve the Lord no matter what. Whatever you lose for Christ, He is able to restore a hundredfold. He can do exceedingly, abundantly above all that we hope or think (see Ephesians 3:20). As for me and my house, we will serve the Lord (see Joshua 24:15). Though none go with me, still, I will follow.

OVERCOMING MANIPULATION

*The fear of man brings a snare,
But whoever trusts in the LORD shall be safe.*
— Proverbs 29:25

A snare is a trap for catching birds or small animals. After that it's dinner time. The fear of man will cause you to be ensnared and consequently never fulfill what God has for you. I went to a birthday party for a young lady who just turned eighteen years old. In her card, I was led by the Spirit to give her the Bible verse Psalm 118:18. It was a prophetic moment that on her eighteenth birthday God would give me this verse for her. *"It is better to trust in the LORD than to put confidence in man."* God was speaking to her very strongly about not waiting around for a young man to take care of her. She was to trust in God and follow His will for her life. In going hard after God she would run straight into the right man for her. Now she is happily married and fulfilling her dreams because she trusted God and courageously marched forward instead of waiting for a man to save her. Don't let anyone hold you back. Whether it's the fear of what others think, or fear of being alone. Trust the Lord; He will never let you down.

There are several manipulation tactics that people use to control others. Some folks have no problem causing others to be co-dependent on them for constant approval. I think all of us have attempted manipulation at times, but with some it's a lifestyle (can you say "cult leader"?). It's never right to bully others, or use your influence to control people for selfish gain.

After reading these I'm sure you will begin to spot them. To be forewarned is to be forearmed. I can't resist being a little humorous about some of these. I figure it's better to laugh about it than to cry.

1. Pack the bags, we're going on a guilt trip: A little guilt and condemnation can go a long way. The devil has been using guilt, shame and condemnation to hold people back for eons. Don't receive a guilt trip, even if you're guilty. If you've done something wrong, get right with God, or apologize to someone. If they don't receive your apology, then it's on them. Don't let anyone manipulate you and beat you over the head with guilt. If I've made things right with the Lord, I will not receive any condemnation. I just won't let it stick.

- Number one: Confess your sins to God. "*If we confess our sins, He is faithful and just to forgive us our sins and to cleanse us from all unrighteousness*" *(I John 1:9).*

- Number two: Confess that you are the righteousness of God in Christ Jesus (see 2 Corinthians 5:21).

- Number three: Try to be at peace with all people. "**If it is possible, as much as depends on you***, live peaceably with all men*" *(Romans 12:18).* If I have tried my best to make things right with people and they insist on tweaking me with guilt, I just won't receive it. I ignore all attempts. Don't give power to the guilt pusher. They will figure out sooner or later that guilt trips don't work on you.

2. Call the whaaaaambulence, I'm a whiner and a pouter: Whining never works on God. It may have worked on your parents but God is not about to empower a bunch of whiners.

There is a difference between a legitimate cry of pain and someone who is never thankful and always whining. God responds to real cries for help and the prayer of faith (see Hebrews 11:6, Psalm 50:13). According to the Bible, incessant complaining killed some folks in their wilderness journey.

> Nor let us tempt Christ, as some of them also tempted, and were destroyed by serpents; **nor complain, as some of them also complained, and were destroyed by the destroyer.** Now all these things happened to them as examples, and they were written for our admonition, upon whom the ends of the ages have come.
> — I Corinthians 10:9-11

Nothing causes leaders to dig in their heels more than when folks try whining to get their way. Also, there is nothing worse than fully grown adults sulking and pouting like a toddler. There is a difference between someone who is despondent because of a terrible situation in his life, and a person trying to manipulate others by pouting. By caving in, and giving them their way, you are not doing them any favors; you are just reinforcing bad behavior. If you are a spiritual leader and give pouters their way, you are inadvertently teaching them that God responds to pouting as well. When people try the pout tactic on me, I ignore it until they get tired. It's that simple.

3. I will throw a fit. We do not negotiate with terrorists: Some folks throw a hissy fit if they don't get their way. When Mount Vesuvius erupts everyone cowers in fear, or so they think. "Give me my way or I will explode!" is the policy of these terrorist bullies. Unfortunately, the only thing a bully understands is a bigger bully. You must take your stand and not be pushed around. They must learn that the intimidation tactic will work against them as privileges and positions are stripped away from them because of their manipulative rage episodes. If you are in a leadership position over these terrorists, you need to stand up to them before things get out of hand. Answer them softly and continue to stand your ground and say no (see Proverbs 15:1). Allowing a rage-oholic to get his/her way reinforces bad toddler behavior. If you are under the authority of someone with rage problems, living under the tyranny and stress of Al Capone is not cool. It's time to plan your escape and get away. If you are married to someone that has lost control, encourage some pastoral counseling, or anger management therapy (not kidding, someone could get hurt). There are legitimate reasons to get angry, but even then you must always exert self-control. But throwing a fit to bully and manipulate is never right. The book of Proverbs has many things to say about anger, and all of us need to take heed.

The Word of God has the power to help us bring anger under control. I believe the Word of God is seed, and if you continue planting it on the good soil of a yielded heart, it will bring a bountiful harvest of righteousness. Plant scriptures every day about anger and its negative effects on you and others. Seek God about root causes and He will help you bring things under control. As believers, we have the Holy Spirit inside of us, and part of the fruit of the Spirit is self-control (see Galatians 5:22-23, John 14:15-18). A bad temper is a life pattern and formed habit; a pattern can be broken and changed.

> *So then, my beloved brethren, let every man be swift to hear, slow to speak, slow to wrath; for the wrath of man does not produce the righteousness of God.*
> *— James 1:19-20*

> *He who is slow to anger is better than the mighty,*
> *And he who rules his spirit than he who takes a city.*
> *— Proverbs 16:32*

> *Make no friendship with an angry man, and with a furious man do not go,*
> *Lest you learn his ways and set a snare for your soul.*
> *— Proverbs 22:24-25*

4. Flattery: You're the best thing since the invention of peanut butter.

> *A man who flatters his neighbor spreads a net for his feet.*
> *— Proverbs 29:5*

There is a difference between flattery and the gift of encouragement in the Bible (see Romans 12:6-8). Godly encouragement is sincere and uplifting. It is pure of heart and has the best interest of others at heart. Encouragers seek to motivate people to their highest potential in Christ. Flattery, on the other hand, seeks to manipulate others for selfish gain or personal advancement. There was a man in the book of Acts nicknamed "Barnabas," which means "son of encouragement." The Bible says that he was a good man, full of the Holy Spirit and faith who encouraged believers in the church of Antioch, that with purpose of heart they should continue with the Lord (see Acts 11:22-24). Barnabas spoke the truth and encouraged others in right living. The book of Jeremiah tells of flattering prophets who told people what they wanted to hear to make them feel good.

> *Thus says the LORD of hosts:*
> *"Do not listen to the words of the prophets who prophesy to you. They make you worthless; they speak a vision of their own*

> *heart, not from the mouth of the LORD.*
> *They continually say to those who despise Me, the LORD*
> *has said, 'You shall have peace;' and to everyone who walks*
> *according to the dictates of his own heart, they say,*
> *'No evil shall come upon you.'"*
> *— Jeremiah 23:16-17*

True exhortation speaks the truth in love. It's not about telling folks what they want to hear to gain acceptance from them. Basically, there are three reasons a person tells faltering lies:

- One, they are deceived and fully believe in the lies they are saying. Have you ever watched one of those reality singing contests on T.V. where the vocalist is surrounded by a mother or friends pumping them up in the lie that they can sing? After they embarrass themselves by singing like a strangled cat, the deceived entourage of flatterers keeps encouraging them to seek fame as a singer! Unbelievably, the self-deceived singer continues to believe lies that his warped fan club tells him. This is what I call "death by entourage."

- Two, they want acceptance so much that they tell people what they want to hear all the time.

- Or three, they are truly twisted and are boldly trying to set you up to take advantage of you. Most of the time folks sincerely love you and want to compliment you, but once in a while the discernment buzzer starts going off in your spirit. BEEP, BEEP, BEEP, FLATTERER! WHAT DO THEY WANT?

If you want to be free from manipulation from flatterers, you must be brutally honest with yourself about how you receive compliments. Are you going through a low and everything about you advertises, "I need someone to tell me how great I am!" Everyone goes through emotional lows; this is where we are vulnerable. Many times, people can never give you the encouragement and self-esteem boost you may crave. We must learn to hear the encouragement of the Holy Spirit. God encourages me when no one else can. My wife catches me fishing for compliments every once in a while. She will tell me how unattractive it is (ouch). I will say things like, "Wow, God really met us in that service this morning." To which the oblivious congregant replies, "He sure did and that sermon was really awesome!" After thanking them for their kind words, I swagger off. Another terrible way to react when someone compliments you is to say something like, "Oh, don't praise me, praise Jesus!" You need to drop the humility act; we all know it's false. Do you think we are tempted to put you right up there next to Jesus and get confused as to who we should worship? Somewhere along the line, you were taught to never receive a compliment or you are in pride. Just say **thank you**. Don't reprimand people for complimenting you. If you make people feel good for complimenting you, they just might want to do it again.

5. "We all think": Do what I say because everyone agrees with me.

> *Everyone proud in heart is an abomination to the LORD;*
> *Though they join forces, none will go unpunished.*
> *— Proverbs 16:5*

Another form of manipulation is when someone pulls the democracy card. They will tell you that "everyone thinks so," or "we all feel." They are trying to put political pressure on you. "We took a poll and everyone agrees with me." Usually it's just two other people and a cat that feel the same way. You need to call their bluff and don't be buffaloed. You should always listen to concerns, but shouldn't succumb to mob pressure. Some feel that everything has to go through the democratic process. If we had to vote on every issue nothing would get done. If there are serious issues, and the bylaws of your organization require a vote by a board or membership, then by all means vote. But when people pull the democracy card over every situation then it's a control issue; by that I mean – who is really in control? When the mob rules, then the person in control is the person influencing the mob.

In Numbers 16, there was a major rebellion that rose up against Moses and Aaron. The ring leader was a man named Korah. Korah approached Moses with a mob of disgruntled leaders, and when you examine what he said to Moses in verse 3, you can see that his argument went like this:

- "Who put you in charge?" A direct challenge to authority.
- "The people should have more of a say." The person influencing the mob wants more power.
- "We are all holy and equal. No one should be above anyone else." We are all equally loved by God but we do not have equal authority. Some will always have more responsibility than others and should be honored for their service.

Let's think about what was really going on here. Do you think the ring leader is seriously concerned with the will of the people? NO! He is concerned about his own will. He wants to be the person in charge and he is using a mob to overthrow the existing regime. If Moses and Aaron had stepped down, would the people have then been in charge? No, they would have elected a new leader, and who would have been nominated? Korah! They would have replaced righteous men of God for a ruthless despot.

If a rebellious person rises to a position of authority, he becomes worse than all the authority he has ever criticized. He will be brutally dominating and overbearing. When it became crystal clear that Moses and Aaron did not appoint themselves over the congregation, but were appointed by God, then the power of the mob spirit dissipated. If you are in a position of authority, hold your ground; you will see that God is with you and stands behind His delegated authority. The "we all think" people find out that they don't have as much influence as they thought, especially when they see good folks stand behind God-appointed leadership. Having several followers doesn't make you right. "*Though they join forces, they will not go unpunished*" *(see Proverbs 11:21).*

These are just some of the obvious manipulation tactics that people use on almost a sub-conscience level. It is our nature to influence, control, and bend others to our will. When we talk about resisting manipulation, we shouldn't allow ourselves to become paranoid. Some people are very passionate about having their opinion heard. We should always give people the courtesy of hearing them out. Good advice is not manipulation.

I have four beautiful daughters. Once I overheard two of them playfully bragging about how they could get their Dad to do almost anything by charming him. It would become a fun game that would reach almost legendary proportions. They would start by telling me what a great dad I was, and then they would tell me how much they loved me. They were much too clever to ask me for something right away, so they would come back again, after those words of affirmation sunk in, and then ask me for something. I always knew exactly what was going on but I loved to watch them play their game. And I have to admit, even knowing that I was being played like a Stradivarius violin I found it difficult to resist their charms. The other technique that was far more effective than flattery was when they turned on the tears. Seeing your little girl crying just melts a dad's heart. I think they could rule the world someday.

OVERCOMING THE FEAR OF RELIGIOUS CHURCH PEOPLE

> *Nevertheless even among the rulers many believed in Him,*
> *but because of the Pharisees they did not confess Him,*
> *lest they should be put out of the synagogue; for they*
> *loved the praise of men more than the praise of God.*
> — John 12:42-43

Never underestimate the power of stupid people in a group. Religious tradition has a powerful hold on people who are uncomfortable with any kind of change. If you rock the boat with even a small wake of suspected change, the delicate constitution of stark religionists will have a rumbly in their tumbly. There will be times when you have to choose between the rightly divided Word of God and the traditions of men. I cannot begin to tell you about the amount of pressure these people can bring to bear on anyone who will dare challenge the status quo.

A young married couple sat down to a nice ham dinner. The ham came steaming out of the oven basted with a glaze of brown sugar and butter. The pineapples that had been impaled into the ham with toothpicks were slightly browned, and the husband asked his wife, "Why do you cut the ends off the ham before you bake it?" She hadn't even thought about that before; she had never even questioned it. "You know," she said, "I always saw my mother do that so I assumed it let the flavor in the sides of the ham. Let me call Mom and ask her." Mom's response was, "I never questioned it, I saw my mother cutting the ends off and thought the reason was because she wanted to make sure the inside of the ham would be cooked, through and through. I will call Grandma and ask her." Grandma replied with a snicker, "I don't know why you girls cut the ends off, but I did it so the ham would fit in the pan." This illustrates that sometimes the usefulness and practicality of certain things no longer exist and we do things mindlessly out of tradition.

One day I was driving my car and listening to Christian radio, and a Bible teacher was answering questions live on the air (sometimes a dangerous thing). The aggravated caller told the host of the radio show that he did not agree with him on so many issues and one of them was infant baptism. The caller was very passionate that all babies should be baptized. The Bible teacher was very calm and asked, "I'll tell you what; you show me a Bible verse that instructs us to baptize babies and I'll show you one that doesn't." The caller responded with, "*Jesus said, 'Suffer the little children to come unto me, and forbid them not: for of such is the kingdom of God*" *(Mark 10:14b)*. The radio host countered, "*There once was a man in the land of Uz, whose name was Job*" *(Job 1:1a)*. The caller quickly asked incredulously, "What does your scripture have to do with infant baptism?" The radio host quipped, "What does YOUR scripture have to do with infant baptism???" At this point,

I had to pull the car over to the side of the road because I was laughing so hard, I am sure I would have been pulled over for drunk driving. The point is that we should make sure what we believe is grounded in the Bible and not in the traditions of men.

The Bible instructs us to, *"Test all things; hold fast to what is good"* (1 Thessalonians 5:21). Faith and practice should be held up to the Bible. *"To the law and to the testimony! If they do not speak according to this word, it is because there is no light in them"* (Isaiah 8:20). Always remember that the measuring rod for truth is the full council of God in the Bible, not the opinions of men who twist the words of God to conform to their vain theories.

> *Then the brethren immediately sent Paul and Silas away by night to Berea. When they arrived, they went into the synagogue of the Jews. These were more fair-minded than those in Thessalonica, in that they received the word with all readiness, and searched the Scriptures daily to find out whether these things were so.*
> — Acts 17:10-11

The Bereans measured what Paul said by the Word of God. They didn't interview the Jews in Thessalonica to see what they thought. The Internet abounds with heresy hunters these days. You can find opposing, and often times whacky views on just about anything. If you have achieved modest notoriety you have become a target of the, DUM, DA DUM DUM, DUMMMMM... Heresy Hunters. These websites fester with outright lies and distorted facts. They take partial sayings and videos out of context and build the most amazing conspiracy theories. Anyone influential enough to make a blip on the radar of fame, and who is making a difference in the Kingdom of God, is on their hit list. If you feed continually on these websites, you will slide into such paranoia that you will trust no one except the heresy hunter for truth. It's not wrong to look at the opinion of others, but what about God's opinion? What about looking at the doctrinal statement of the ministry being attacked and comparing that with the Word of God? Like I said, the Bereans did not go by the opinions of the Jews in Thessalonica who ran Paul out of town; they looked intently and tested Paul's doctrine by the Word of God. Instead of needing to have the constant approval of the self-appointed heresy police in the Body of Christ, learn to think for yourself. Instead of listening to what everybody else says about a ministry, watch a podcast or YouTube video. Go to their website and see what their doctrinal statement is.

There is a difference between someone in denial of central doctrine, and people not liking laughter, miracles, or the gifts of the Holy Spirit (see 1 Corinthians 12:7-11). There are two simple questions you have to ask: 1) What is their central doctrine, and especially, what is their doctrine of Christ (see 2 John 9-10)? By "doctrine of Christ" I mean: He is eternally God, co-equal with the Father and the Holy Spirit. He humbled Himself and became a man, born of a virgin, lived a sinless life, died vicariously for our sins, rose from the dead and sits at the right hand of God, He is coming again physically to set up His earthly reign on earth and to judge the world. 2) What is the fruit of their ministry? By "fruit" I mean, what do they produce? Are people legitimately being set free and giving glory to God? Are folks coming into maturity and being fruitful in a local church? And so forth...

You can't let religious dead heads stop you from going forward in good wholesome teaching and fresh renewal. You must march on in your spiritual growth. You will be tested. Do you love the praises of men more than the praises of God? You are responsible for YOU. It's time to come into maturity and know what you believe. You must reach the point where you are confident to discern truth. You must know the scriptures for yourself. *"To the law and to the testimony! If they do not speak according to this word, it is because there is no light in them"* (Isaiah. 8:20).

OVERCOMING THE FEAR OF FAMILY

He who loves father or mother more than Me is not worthy of Me. And he who loves son or daughter more than Me is not worthy of Me. And he who does not take his cross and follow after Me is not worthy of Me.
— *Matthew 10:37-38*

The above Bible verse is one of those hard sayings of Jesus. He is NOT telling us to neglect or be unloving to our family (see 1 Timothy 5:8). He IS telling us that when push comes to shove, you must choose Jesus over your family. You cannot let your family obstruct your faith and keep you from following Jesus. How does this flesh out? Simply put, when you have to choose between pleasing your family or doing the will of God, you should obey God.

Family falls into two categories: The nuclear family and the extended family. A nuclear family is a father and mother (married man and woman) with dependent children. The extended family is everyone else related to you. The dynamics in the nuclear family are more complex than the extended family, so we will deal with the extended family first.

THE EXTENDED FAMILY

> *Then His brothers and His mother came, and standing outside they sent to Him, calling Him. And a multitude was sitting around Him; and they said to Him, "Look, Your mother and Your brothers are outside seeking You." But He answered them, saying, "Who is My mother, or My brothers?" And He looked around in a circle at those who sat about Him, and said, "Here are My mother and My brothers! For whoever does the will of God is My brother and My sister and mother."*
> *— Mark 3:31-35*

I don't think we have to go through a complicated exegesis of these scriptures to see clearly what Jesus is saying. The bottom line is that when your extended family is hindering you from obeying God and His Word, you are obligated to obey God rather than blood related family. This is crystal clear in cases where becoming a follower of Jesus means being disowned and ostracized by extended family. The water becomes muddied where commitment to family events becomes nothing short of idolatry. By idolatry I mean, holding something in higher esteem than God; letting something have more influence over you than God.

As a pastor I see many struggles people have with their extended family. In some cases, the extended family doesn't like the commitment you have made to Jesus. They think it's too extreme. "Moderation" is the overused buzz word used to criticize your commitment to Jesus. They think you're too fanatical because you go to church twice a week, read your Bible and are not at every family event. Other times, the extended family is upset that you have left the traditional family church for a church more alive. There is a cost for following Jesus. Sometimes it can be very painful when you are persecuted by family for your love and need for God. Don't give up. If you are rejected by family for Christ, God raises up surrogate grandparents in the body of Christ; surrogate fathers, mothers, brothers and sisters. It is so beautiful seeing the love of God displayed through the Body of Christ (see Mark 10:29-31).

> So Jesus answered and said, "Assuredly, I say to you, there is no one who has left house or brothers or sisters or father or mother or wife or children or lands, for My sake and the gospel's, who shall not receive a hundredfold now in this time—houses and brothers and sisters and mothers and children and lands, with persecutions—and in the age to come, eternal life.
> — Mark 10:29-30

> God sets the solitary in families; He brings out those who are bound into prosperity; But the rebellious dwell in a dry land.
> — Psalms 68:6

There was a family that I pastored that had cousins by the dozens. It seemed they could only make one church service a month because the family was always having birthday parties on Sundays. Finally, they just had to tell their family members that they would be late for these events because they had committed to their local church. How do you think that went over? Like a lead balloon! Sooner or later you must make proper boundaries with your extended family. Going to birthday parties late is hardly being neglectful of family responsibilities.

THE NUCLEAR FAMILY

The nuclear family is a married father and mother with dependent children. Also included in this category would be a single mother or father with dependent children.

Children:

> *Children, obey your parents in the Lord, for this is right. "Honor your father and mother," which is the first commandment with promise: "that it may be well with you and you may live long on the earth."*
> *— Ephesians 6:1-3*

We have had many outreaches through our church that targeted children. Many children would make a commitment to follow Christ and want to come to church and be baptized. Parents were often supportive but once in a while they would be hostile to their children serving Christ and going to a Christian church. A girl wrote me a letter once begging me to talk to her folks because they wouldn't let her come to church. I did talk to them but to no avail. They were quite adamant that they had no intention of letting any of their children go to church or get baptized. What is a person under 17 or 18 years of age supposed to do under these circumstances?

First, we would get them their own Bible (age appropriate) and devotional material so they could continue to pursue Christ on their own. Second, we would hook them up with Christian friends who would encourage them in their walk. There might even be a Bible club at school they can attend. Third, we would encourage them to be obedient to their parents in all things, except when the parents asked them to stop following Jesus.

This can be very challenging to a young person, especially when parents are encouraging them to do things against their new faith. I knew a dad that took his son out on his sixteenth birthday intending to get his son drunk and to buy him a prostitute. In this father's mind, this was how his son would come into manhood. The son refused and was ridiculed to scorn. No matter what age you are, becoming a disciple of Jesus takes guts. You may even risk defying some crazy family ritual.

It's important to be a good witness for your faith. If the young person works hard in school and has a good attitude about helping at home, this speaks volumes. Honoring and loving your parents as best you can will adorn the Gospel and hopefully demonstrate to the parents that serving Jesus is beneficial.

Husbands and wives:

> *Nevertheless let each one of you in particular so love his own wife as himself, and let the wife see that she respects her husband.*
> *— Ephesians 5:33*

What do you do if your spouse is not serving the Lord, or if he/she is walking away from their relationship with Christ and trying to drag you with them? The bottom line is that you mustn't let anyone come between you and your relationship with the Lord. I can't address every possible scenario that can take place in a marriage. Suffice it to say that it all comes down to love and respect. If you do your utmost to be loving and respectful to your spouse, there is a good chance he/she will follow you into your faith in Christ. But even if he/she does not follow you, you must go forward. Try to be the best witness you can be and adorn your faith in Christ with honorable behavior. As much as you want your spouse to be a co-laborer with you in Christ, you must do everything in your power to be patient and loving. No one can force or manipulate another person to be a sincere follower of Christ. Because your spouse is an unbeliever and does not want to become a Christian, this is not in itself an excuse to divorce them.

This is what the Apostle Paul has to say on this issue:

> *But to the rest I, not the Lord, say: If any brother has a wife who does not believe, and she is willing to live with him, let him not divorce her. And a woman who has a husband who does not believe, if he is willing to live with her, let her not divorce him.*
> *— 1 Corinthians 7:12-13*

There are three scriptural reasons for divorce. I call them the triple A's of divorce: *Abandonment* (see 1 Corinthians 7:15), *adultery* (see Matthew 19:9), and *abuse*. In extreme situations I always recommend separation. No one should have to stay in a situation where they are physically or emotionally abused. If none of these triple A's are happening, you must fight in the spirit for the salvation of your spouse. You must fight in the natural by demonstrating a wholesome lifestyle. You must do everything on your part to be loving and show respect. If your spouse is not a believer and supports your decision to serve Jesus, you are obligated by the Word of God to NOT seek divorce. Like I said, I can't answer every question and possible scenario, please seek qualified counseling. I will state one thing clearly though, don't let anyone stop you from following Jesus.

> *Let no one cheat you of your reward.*
> *— Colossians 2:18a*

> *Look to yourselves, that we do not lose those things we worked for, but that we may receive a full reward.*
> *— 2 John 8be*

No relationship on this planet is worth losing your reward. As painful as it is to let people go and stay walking with Christ, many times it cannot be helped. Rising above needing the acceptance and praise of man can be the test of a lifetime. It can also be very liberating to not be swayed by every whim and wish of people. It's only by the grace of God that we can be strong and stay the course. Above all else we must look to the reward. "He is a rewarder of those who diligently serve Him" (Hebrews 11:6b).

> *I would have lost heart, unless I had believed*
> *That I would see the goodness of the LORD*
> *In the land of the living.*
> *— Psalm 27:13*

Chapter 9

Guarding Against Sexual Lust

*For by means of a harlot a man is reduced to a crust of bread;
and an adulteress will prey upon his precious life.
Can a man take fire to his bosom, and his clothes not be burned?
Can one walk on hot coals, and his feet not be seared?
So is he who goes in to his neighbor's wife; whoever touches
her shall not be innocent.*
— Proverbs 6:26-29

We live in a society that is over crazed and obsessed with sex. Let's face it, sex sells. The pornography industry is a multi-billion-dollar, tax-exempt, international cesspool. When you drive down the street, soft porn is on billboards. When you turn on the television, images abound. I can be watching a G or PG-rated show with my family and a soft porn commercial will pop up at every intermission. What kind of television producer allows R-rated commercials during a PG-rated show? There are little or no enforced guidelines. I can be walking in the local mall and displays of beautiful women in lingerie abound. If my wife is with me she will apologize and block my view. What's a guy with testosterone enriched blood supposed to do?? Even in church, modesty is not displayed by some of our young women. I have to depend on some of our matriarchal ladies to attempt discipleship with the young women. It IS possible for men and women to dress fashionably, modestly, and not look prudish.

Not only does sex sell, but promiscuous sexual behavior is dangerous. Sexually transmitted diseases abound causing a lifetime of pain, infertility and, in some cases, death. Africa has been facing an AIDS (Auto Immune Deficiency Syndrome) pandemic for many years causing millions of orphaned children. These children are highly at risk and vulnerable. Many are scooped up by sex traffickers and militia groups. Not to mention the negative psychological effects of sexual promiscuity: broken hearts, depression, suicide, low self-esteem or no self-esteem. And one of the worst side effects is a hard heart about sex that when carried into a marriage causes great dysfunction. What's really scary is the seared conscience towards casual sexual encounters. Can you imagine someone walking up to you and saying, "Sorry I slept with your spouse, it just happened. I hope this won't affect our friendship"?

> *This is the way of an adulterous woman: She eats and wipes her mouth, and says, "I have done no wickedness."*
> *— Proverbs 30:20*

I was the chaplain for a Christian High School and I had a Bible study that some could take for credit. I began a series on sexuality and the Bible. I opened with the following scripture:

> *For this is the will of God, your sanctification: that you should abstain from **sexual immorality;** that each of you should know how to possess his own vessel in sanctification and honor, not in passion of lust, like the Gentiles who do not know God; that no one should take advantage of and defraud his brother in this matter,* ***because the Lord is the avenger of all such****, as we*

> *also forewarned you and testified. For God did not call us to uncleanness, but in holiness. Therefore he who rejects this does not reject man, but God, who has also given us His Holy Spirit.*
> — 1 Thessalonians 4:3-8

I began explaining to my class of teenagers that the words "sexual immorality" in some other translations is the word "fornication." In the Greek language, this word is "porneia" (see Strong's Concordance #4202) from which we get the words "pornography" and "pornographic". This word describes illicit sexual intercourse, prostitution, incest, bestiality, adultery, homosexuality, and habitual immorality like addiction to pornography. Basically, any sexual behavior outside of a marriage relationship between a man and a woman is porneia and is a sin according to God's Word.

The majority of the class was blown away. They had no idea that sex outside of marriage was WRONG! They all agreed that adultery was wrong and once you are married you should stay true to your spouse, but why was sex before marriage wrong? As a Bible teacher, I assumed that everyone knew that sex outside of a marriage covenant was wrong, so I was kinda blown away by this reaction.

> *Marriage is honorable among all, and the bed undefiled; but fornicators and adulterers God will judge.*
> — Hebrews 13:4

To say that trying to stay pure in this present age is a "challenge" is a gross understatement. We definitely need the grace of God and the self-control of the Holy Spirit. Temptation abounds and even some of the most unlikely candidates have succumbed. Each of us can point to a person that we thought was a paradigm of virtue only to see them dragged through the mud pit of shame and controversy as sexual indiscretions were brought to light.

> Now therefore, listen to me, my children; Pay attention to the words of my mouth: Do not let your heart turn aside to her ways, do not stray into her paths; **For she has cast down many wounded, and all who were slain by her were strong men.** Her house is the way to hell, descending to the chambers of death.
> — Proverbs 7:24-27

In the first nine chapters of Proverbs, King Solomon personifies the way of wisdom as a virtuous woman calling to all the simpletons to learn. The way of folly and destruction is personified by a whorish woman who is in every marketplace trying to seduce all who pass by. The seductive power of sexual lust has cast down many wounded, all who were slain by her were strong men. If you would like to avoid the destructive minefields that have destroyed many lives and ministries, then I have some good advice.

A HEALTHY MARRIAGE IS GOD'S PROTECTION

> Nevertheless, because of sexual immorality, let each man have his own wife, and let each woman have her own husband.
> — 1 Corinthians 7:2

> ...if they cannot exercise self-control, let them marry. For it is better to marry than to burn with passion.
> — 1 Corinthians 7:9

God created marriage as the ultimate expression of sexual romance. The greatest protection against sexual immorality is a wholesome marriage. When you read these verses as a stand-alone synopsis on marriage, you may think that marriage is a dull, clinical exercise in procreation and nothing more. When we study the Bible, we need to look at all of God's counsel on marriage, from the entire book. The Bible has a lot to say about romance and marital bliss. A healthy and enduring marriage is an effective shield against sexual immorality.

A healthy marriage has five major components that will ensure a growing love and fulfilled life together: 1) love for God, 2) love and respect for one another, 3) romance, 4) friendship, and 5) commitment.

1. Love for God: A person who loves God and maintains a hunger for Him is very attractive. Though a woman's physical beauty may fade, when she fears the Lord she shall be praised (see Proverbs 31:30). I often advise young Christian men to find a wife who loves the Lord as much or more than they do, because she will be faithful and willing to work through problems out of her love for the Lord. Love for God and being individually committed to growing in Christ is paramount to a successful marriage. If you feel that your spouse is not committed to growing spiritually, please persevere and pray for them.

2. Love and respect: Living close to others will cause you to see them at their best and worst. You must make a conscious decision to maintain respect and love. Tell your spouse you love him/her often. Be careful with harsh criticism. If your spouse is a seeker of God, the Lord will speak to him/her about issues that need changing. I'm not saying that we should never discuss negative issues with our spouses, but a constant barrage of degrading criticism is an overkill. We need to be praying for each other more than criticizing and being nit-picky. Never openly criticize your spouse in front of others. There is nothing more gross and awkward than being forced to listen to someone shaming their spouse. When you show appreciation and love for your mate, it will bring out the best in them and cause him/her to achieve great heights. Your mate's prosperity is your prosperity. You're not in competition with each other. Compliment often. Be a mutual admiration society.

3. Romance: When you are in pursuit of God and love and respect each other, great sexual romance is sure to follow. It's hard to have good sex when you've just taken all the stresses of life out on your spouse. Don't wait for your mate to do what's right; you start sowing good things into your marriage by complimenting often and telling your spouse that you love him/her. My wife asked me if I was ever tempted and I replied, "Why do I want to drive a cheap compact car when I have a Porsche at home?"

4. Friendship: The Song of Solomon is God's love book. It's not just a spiritual analogy of Christ's love for the church. It also proves that God approves of and created romantic love. "*His mouth is most sweet, yes, he is altogether lovely. This is my beloved, and this is my friend*" (Song of Solomon 5:16). My wife is my best friend. Once in a while we need a break from each other, but we LIKE to be with each other. I had a friend comment that we do almost everything together' he was suggesting that perhaps that wasn't healthy. My response was that we want to be with each other. My wife is my best friend as well as my lover. If you would like your friendship with your spouse to grow, find things they like to do and join in. My wife is into flowers, I am not. But I started going to nurseries with her and wouldn't you know it, I started looking forward to it. A friendship is about finding common ground.

5. Commitment: There must be a commitment and a sense of responsibility for each other. We never threaten each other with divorce. We are committed to making our relationship work. Your marriage can be a living hell, or it can be enjoyable and fun. We decide how we want to live. My attitude and commitment to love and respect my spouse will determine the quality of my life.

If you are experiencing a great challenge in your marriage right now, please don't be discouraged by anything I've written here. Press into the Lord. Pray and seek help. You can have a loving and successful marriage. *"With men it is impossible, but with God all things are possible" (Mark 10:27).*

Paul prophesied that in later times they would forbid to marry (see 1 Timothy 4:1-5). You can see this coming to pass because of the savage times we are living in. People can be very narcissistic, harsh and covenant breaking. Some are legitimate victims in a ME-oriented lawless, godless society. Because of the tragic carnage left in the wake of destroyed marriages, many jaded souls have opted out of marriage and have embraced cohabitation. Living together carries its own set of problems. It will not cure the problems of failed marriages, it just adds more; it creates insecurity and makes it easier to separate. The problem is not with the institution of marriage, it's with our lost and broken hearts. We need the power of God more than ever to establish lasting, loving relationships.

STUMBLING AND PRACTICING
ARE TWO DIFFERENT THINGS

Do you not know that the unrighteous will not inherit the kingdom of God? ***Do not be deceived.*** *Neither fornicators, nor*

> *idolaters, nor adulterers, nor homosexuals, nor sodomites, nor thieves, nor covetous, nor drunkards, nor revilers, nor extortioners **will inherit the kingdom of God.** And such were some of you. But you were washed, but you were sanctified, but you were justified in the name of the Lord Jesus and by the Spirit of our God.*
> — *1 Corinthians 6:9-11*

There is nothing that the blood of Jesus cannot wash us from. There is nothing that cannot be forgiven through repentance and faith in the atoning death of Jesus on the cross. When you are a new creation in Christ you are made new, old things have passed away (see 2 Corinthians 5:17). If you stumble and sin you can appeal to God's merciful forgiveness (see 1 John 2:1-2), but if you continue in a lifestyle of sexual immorality you will not make heaven: you will go to hell. What do you think it means when the Bible says that "the unrighteous will not inherit the kingdom of God"? It's not talking about a person who stumbles, falls and gets back up (see Proverbs 24:16, Psalm 37:23-24), it's talking about someone deceiving themselves and continuing in a lifestyle of sin.

If you are in a sexual relationship with someone outside of marriage you must break it off or get married. If you are living together and have been avoiding marriage, get married quickly or break it off. If you are addicted to pornography, you need to burn all bridges to temptation and seek a confidential accountability group immediately. This is serious business with God! This is a heaven or hell issue!

> ***Flee sexual immorality.*** *Every sin that a man does is outside the body, but he who commits sexual immorality sins against his own body. Or do you not know that your body is the temple of the Holy Spirit who is in you, whom you have from God, and you*

> are not your own? For you were bought at a price; therefore
> glorify God in your body and in your spirit, which are God's.
> — 1 Corinthians 6:18-20

> For this you know, that no fornicator, unclean person,
> nor covetous man, who is an idolater, has any inheritance
> in the kingdom of Christ and God. **Let no one deceive you
> with empty words,** for because of these things the
> wrath of God comes upon the sons of disobedience.
> Therefore do not be partakers with them.
> — Ephesians 5:5-7

TEMPTATION IS NOT SIN

> For we do not have a High Priest who cannot sympathize
> with our weaknesses, but was in all points tempted
> as we are, yet without sin.
> — Hebrews 4:15

Temptation is not sin. Jesus was tempted but did not sin. Whenever we are tempted, Jesus can help us because He was tempted in all points as we are (see Hebrews 2:18). I have known many men, myself included, who have been tormented with condemnation because of fleeting thoughts and temptations. I have heard it said that you can't stop the birds from flying over your head, but you can keep them from nesting in your hair. Fleeting feelings and thoughts come and go, but when you let that temptation take root and decide in your heart that given the chance you will act on it, then it is sin.

> Let no one say when he is tempted, "I am tempted by God"; for
> God cannot be tempted by evil, nor does He Himself
> tempt anyone. But each one is tempted when he is
> drawn away by his own desires and enticed. Then,

> *when desire has conceived, it gives birth to sin; and sin,
> when it is full-grown, brings forth death.*
> — James 1:13-15

Notice the progression here; temptation turns into desire, desire gives birth to sin, and when sin is full-grown it brings forth death. When you allow a temptation to become an overwhelming desire that you will act on if given a chance, then you are in sin. When you act on that desire it will bring forth some kind of death. The principle of death will start to work in your life and relationships. Sin will always bring forth some kind of death and destruction (see Romans 6:23). Through the power of the Holy Spirit, who resides in us as believers, we can cast down every thought and imagination that exalts itself against the knowledge of God (see 2 Corinthians 10:3-5). If we want God's blessing on our relationships, we must repent and forsake all forms of sexual immorality. It's very selfish to push someone into a sexual relationship outside of marriage knowing that it is hurting them and their relationship with God. Last time I checked, love does no harm.

GUARD THE EYE GATE AND THE HEART GATE

The eye gate:

The eye gate and the heart gate are key strategic high grounds that must be protected. Let's discuss the eye gate first. Although men seem to be tempted more visually, and women through the heart and emotions, I find that both men and women struggle in these same areas.

As Christians, we can't just allow ourselves to gawk at the opposite sex. We are called to a higher standard. I took some young men to a football game, and when some attractive young women walked by, they stared and whistled shamelessly. I slapped them alongside the head and said, "What are you doing? Put your eyes back in your head and stop drooling all over yourselves. You are not animals, you are men of God and you will behave like gentlemen."

We must guard what we are seeing with our eyes and turn away from sexual images. Pornographic images are a toxic fuel. It's like throwing kerosene on a fire that is barely being contained as it is. These images are highly addictive, run away! The porn industry knows how addictive these images are and they are cleverly concealing them in innocent places. The first pill is free and then they hope you will be back for more. Block suspicious friend requests on social media. It's not hard to figure out a porn solicitation. As soon as you see the profile pic you should know that the girl named Kitty from Lithuania is not someone you know. Put blocks on TV stations. On my satellite TV network, I can block titles from being seen and block ratings and sexual content. Be sure of this, your sin will find you out. If you would be highly ashamed if caught watching or reading something, then don't do it. If you are caught in the vice of pornography's grip, then find an accountability group before your life is destroyed. Porn is an equal opportunity destroyer. Guard your eye gate fiercely. Don't give in to peer pressure from perverted carnal men who think it's manly to gawk at centerfolds and treat women shamefully. Ask yourself a question, "What kind of young man do I want dating my daughter?" Become that man of honor.

> I DICTATED a covenant (an agreement) to my eyes; how then
> could **I look [lustfully]** upon a girl?
> — Job 31:1 AMP

> *You have heard that it was said, 'Do not commit adultery.' But I
> tell you that anyone who looks at a woman lustfully has already
> committed adultery with her in his heart.*
> — Matthew 5:27-28 NIV

The heart gate:

The next area that needs to be highly guarded is the heart. An adulterous relationship begins mostly with an unwholesome emotional attachment. Either a person is vulnerable or just restless and careless in guarding their affections. Putting appropriate boundaries around your heart is something that must be taught. Many false assumptions are being espoused by the popular media that will lead to destruction.

> *Above all else, guard your heart, for it is the wellspring of life.*
> — Proverbs 4:23 NIV

There seem to be myths about platonic relationships. Platonic relationships with the opposite sex must be guarded. Despite what popular culture tells you, if someone attractive from the opposite sex is your best friend, feelings will most likely develop. If you have to work closely with the opposite sex, you need to put professional boundaries up. If you have close friendships with the opposite sex and then one of your "friends" falls in love with you, you may NOT have a right to be angry. YOU may be to blame. Playing games with the affections of others for ego's sake is a cruel game. Now if someone starts stalking you and you have honestly not led them on, then that's different. If you are married

Guarding Against Sexual Lust

and palling around with people of the opposite sex, you are playing with fire. I don't care how strong you think you are; you are not putting proper boundaries up. You are setting yourself up for a fall. All I am saying is… be careful with platonic relationships.

Another myth is that people will say that they just "fell" into an affair. Or, they couldn't stop their feelings, it just happened. If you will be honest, no one just "falls" into an affair, or love for that matter. God starts warning His children in advance of such trouble. Folks just choose to ignore the warning signs and stubbornly bulldog forward. The heart began to stray way before the affair happened. This is a pre-meditated sin; deliver yourself. *"The backslider in heart will be filled with his own ways, but a good man will be satisfied from above"* (Proverbs 14:14). Backsliding starts in the heart long before the follow-through actions. We must guard our hearts with all diligence, for out of it flows the wellsprings of life (see Proverbs 4:23).

Before you start playing around with the idea of having an affair, STOP and THINK! Think beyond yourself to all of the lives this flesh party will affect. Think of your husband or wife. Think of your children. An affair is an act of violence against your family.

Remember to guard fiercely your eye gate and your heart gate.

SAMSON AND DELILAH

(Please read the story of Samson in Judges 13 – 16)

> *Now all these things happened to them as examples,
> and they were written for our admonition, upon whom the
> ends of the ages have come. Therefore let him who thinks he
> stands take heed lest he fall. No temptation has overtaken
> you except such as is common to man; but God is faithful,
> who will not allow you to be tempted beyond what you are
> able, but with the temptation will also make the way of
> escape, that you may be able to bear it.*
> — 1 Corinthians 10:10-13 NKJV

The Bible is replete with examples of victories and moral failure. The story of Samson is full of admonitions that will help us guard our hearts. Samson was a man of tremendous athletic ability and physical strength, both naturally and supernaturally. The Philistines would not have paid good money to know the secret of Samson's great strength if there wasn't something above and beyond mere natural ability. Just before Samson performed a spectacular feat of strength, the Bible would give this formula, "*Then the Spirit of the Lord came upon him mightily*" (see Judges 14:19, 15:14). To single-handedly wipe out a regiment of 1,000 men with a jaw bone of a donkey in one battle, to rip open the jaws of an attacking lion and sustain no injuries, to pull a heavy brass gate out of a city wall, put it on your back and sprint up a hill with it, and to push apart the foundation pillars of a stadium and crush everyone inside are definitely not normal strong man competition events.

The secret to Samson's great strength was his Nazirite vow to God. A Nazirite was to live a separated life above that of the normal Israelite. He was not to drink any wine or alcoholic drink or ever cut his hair. Even though he kept his vow concerning these issues, he had a weakness that led to his downfall. He was attracted to high-priced ladies of the night. The Bible gives record of two Philistine prostitutes in chapter sixteen of the book of Judges. The second one was a real doozy. Her name was Delilah and she had her own beautiful valley home to entertain clients and was connected to very powerful men of her nation. This woman was so cold-hearted that she was willing to betray her lover to the Philistine lords for a good sum of money. She enticed Samson under the pretense that true love should have no secrets until he finally yielded and revealed the secret to his great strength; his Nazirite vow. If the seven locks of his hair were cut, he would become like any other man.

Isn't this the secret to the Christian's strength? *"The Lord is the strength of my life; of whom shall I be afraid?" (Psalm 27:1b).* Our relationship to God and our separation from this world's vices, by His power, give us longevity and success. We are encouraged to not sacrifice our high calling and succumb to petty carnality. We are set apart for holy use and not for common purposes any longer. Paul exhorts us not to behave like mere men (see 1 Corinthians 3:3). **If there is no difference between us and the world, then there is no difference.**

> *The mouth of an immoral woman is a deep pit;*
> *He who is abhorred by the LORD will fall there.*
> — Proverbs 22:14

Delilah lulled him to sleep and snipped his curly locks, thus breaking the Nazirite vow. Samson didn't even realize that the Spirit of God had left him (see Judges 16:20). Compromise had left him spiritually dull. The Philistines put out his eyes and he became both physically and spiritually blind. Samson was put to work on a grinder in the prison. His high calling was forfeited and he was left on the world's treadmill. Doing the work of a donkey or ox, Samson had played the fool.

A question arises when we consider the downward progression of Samson's life. How could God use him so powerfully while he was cavorting with prostitutes? One thing is for sure, your sin will find you out eventually (see Numbers 32:23). You can sometimes fool yourself into thinking that because lightning from heaven didn't immediately strike you down when you sinned, then it must not be so bad. Or worse yet, God must be okay with my sin. Don't mistake God's patience and longsuffering with apathy.

> *Because the sentence against an evil work is not executed speedily, therefore the heart of the sons of men is fully set in them to do evil.*
> *— Ecclesiastes 8:11*

Spiritual giftedness is not always the best gauge of someone's character. Just because a person prophesies or prays for the sick and sees them healed does not always mean that they are super spiritual. I've seen people move tremendously in the Gifts of the Holy Spirit (see 1 Corinthians 12-14) and their personal lives were in shambles. The word "charismata" used for the Gifts of the Spirit means "grace gifts." They can operate by the grace of God and not on personal holiness. Don't be deceived into thinking that because you or someone else is used powerfully in the spiritual gifts that you have arrived. We are always a work in progress. When you look at the qualifications of Elders and Deacons in 1 Timothy 3, you will not find "moving in the Gifts of the Spirit" as a requirement. It's all about proven character and a consistent lifestyle. Leaders are called to a higher standard. Like the Nazirite vow of old, they are called to a higher consecration, a step up from the baseline requirements to be a follower of Jesus. If it's too hot for you, then get out of the kitchen. If you are unwilling to pay the price of self-denial, then consider what you are doing. A leader's circle of influence creates greater collateral damage and has more far-reaching consequences.

Samson is a good admonition to us about how a little compromise can grow into a weapon of mass destruction. In many cases, the obliteration is so complete that no form of restoration is possible.

> *He who is often rebuked, and hardens his neck,*
> *Will suddenly be destroyed, and that without remedy.*
> *— Proverbs 29:1*

JOSEPH AND POTIPHAR'S WIFE

(Please read the full story of Joseph, Genesis 37, 39-50)

> *Thus he left all that he had in Joseph's hand, and he did not know what he had except for the bread which he ate. Now Joseph was handsome in form and appearance. And it came to pass after these things that his master's wife cast longing eyes on Joseph, and she said, "Lie with me." But he refused and said to his master's wife, "Look, my master does not know what is with me in the house, and he has committed all that he has to my hand. There is no one greater in this house than I, nor has he kept back anything from me but you, because you are his wife. How then can I do this great wickedness, and sin against God?" So it was, as she spoke to Joseph day by day, that he did not heed her, to lie with her or to be with her.*
> *— Genesis 39:6-10*

Joseph is the stellar opposite of Samson. Whereas Samson had mighty giftings from God to lead, his life became a shipwreck; his lack of sexual self-control brought him to ruination on the rocky shore of mocking Philistines. If great gifting is not accompanied by elite character, it becomes wasted. Your gifting can take you places where your lack of character can't keep you.

Joseph was a highly skilled administrator, both naturally and enhanced by God's blessing. "*...the LORD was with him and that the LORD made all he did to prosper in his hand" (Genesis 39:3b)*. When we stay right with God, He can enhance natural gifting and add to it spiritual gifting that complements the work of our hands. In Joseph's case, God not only blessed his administrative gifting but gave him the ability to interpret dreams (see Genesis 40, 41). He knew that sin would corrupt the flow of God's blessings and he was in a desperate place. Sold into slavery by his own brothers, his only hope was to look to God to fulfill His Word, given to him by dreams (see Genesis 37:5-11). Thus is revealed a great secret to staying in the keeping power of God and guarding yourself against sin and compromise; look hopefully for God to fulfill His promises and bring your dream to pass. Maintaining a hopeful expectation in God has keeping power.

If Joseph had lost hope and had nothing to live for, he would have self-destructed. This was not the case. He kept his eye on the vision that God gave him and it provided supreme keeping power. Joseph indicated that the sin of giving in to Potiphar's wife's advances would be against God. He had a higher fear and reverence for God than Potiphar, who had the power to put him to death. Joseph was more respectful of God's power than that of the captain of Pharaoh's guard. As Christians, we have a higher accountability than man's authority on earth; the Almighty is the ultimate authority. When we work, we serve the Lord Jesus and it is He that is the rewarder (see Colossians 3:22-25). If man withholds reward, or if injustice and false accusation occur, we commit our souls to the Judge of all the earth. He will somehow make it right.

Another secret to overcoming sexual temptation in this story is that Joseph didn't play with fire. He avoided Potiphar's wife at all costs. He didn't put himself in tempting situations. A wise man, or woman, acknowledges their weakness. An alcoholic must first acknowledge that he/she has a problem before appropriate steps can be taken to get help. And by all means, they don't hang around in night clubs and bars. Joseph was a handsome young man and at the height of his sex drive. There must have been some temptation there or Joseph wouldn't have been so vigilant to avoid her. What I have found is that common sense isn't very common. Avoid scenarios where you are alone and vulnerable to temptation.

Some time ago a young woman called me sobbing and in tears. I met with her at the local coffee shop and found her very broken-hearted. She was a new Christian and on fire for God and His Word. She went and visited her former live-in boyfriend intending to witness about her new life in Christ. After a good conversation with him, they ended up falling into sin. Ashamed and feeling like a failure, she needed a good word from God. What she didn't need was for someone to condemn her. She was already feeling very low. She loved Jesus with all her heart and wanted just to please Him. After praying, the Lord led me to Psalm 139:17-18, "*How precious also are Your thoughts to me, O God! How great is the sum of them! If I should count them, they would be more in number than the sand; when I awake, I am still with You."*

I told her, "If God thinks more thoughts towards you than there are grains of sand on the seashore, then He must love you an awful lot. He thinks a lot of you." After that, we prayed a prayer of repentance together and the Holy Spirit began to comfort her. I had to give her a word of wisdom though; I convinced her that it was not her responsibility to personally witness to her ex-boyfriend. I said, "We will pray for him and God will be faithful to send witnesses to him. Don't make yourself vulnerable to that toxic relationship again. Give him to the Lord. In God's timing, He will provide the right husband for you. *"Seek first the Kingdom of God and His righteousness, and all these things shall be added to you"* (Matthew 6:33). If you put God and His will first you will run right smack into your husband."

I am so glad that God is there to catch us when we fall. *"If we confess our sins, He is faithful and just to forgive us our sins and to cleanse us from all unrighteousness"* (1 John 1:9).

Joseph passed his test and was ultimately promoted to Pharaoh's court. Before promotion there is always a test. Because Joseph passed his test, his prophetic dreams were realized. Keep your eye on the high calling of God in Christ and avoid compromising situations.

> *Flee also youthful lusts; but pursue righteousness, faith, love, peace with those who call on the Lord out of a pure heart.*
> *— 2 Timothy 2:22*

Guarding Against Sexual Lust

DAVID AND BATHSHEBA

(Please read the book of 2 Samuel)

2 Samuel records the 40-year reign of Israel's most iconic king, King David. His reign is divided into two 20-year periods. The dividing point is his tragic sin of adultery and subsequent murder of Bathsheba's husband Uriah. Before this event, David could do nothing wrong. He went from triumph to triumph. After this event, we begin mourning the tangled tragedies that threatened to unravel the kingdom. David and Bathsheba's firstborn son died, Amnon raped his half-sister Tamar, Tamar's brother Absalom murdered Amnon and was driven into exile; when Absalom was allowed to return he plotted to take the throne and start a civil war. The Kingdom of Israel was almost torn to pieces by the turmoil in David's dysfunctional family.

All of the problems that David and his family faced were the result of his adulterous affair and the murder of Uriah. How do I know this? Because it was prophesied to David by Nathan the prophet (see 2 Samuel 12:9-14). Nathan told him by the Spirit of God that the sword would not depart from his house and that an adversary from his own house would lie with David's wives in the sight of Israel and the sun. David had sinned secretly, but the repercussions would be public. Even though David repented with tears, he could not stop the avalanche of troubles that cascaded upon him and his family as a result of an adulterous affair.

One thing that never ceases to grieve and amaze me is when a man or woman of God has adulterous affairs and then makes a reference to David and Bathsheba. "Well David sinned and God still used him. He was still called a man after

God's own heart." It's as if they somehow think that they are exempt from any negative consequences from their actions and they seem to have selective amnesia concerning all of the tragic events that befell King David as a result of his sin.

The more authority and influence a person may have, the more impacting their negative choices have. The greater the authority, the greater the consequences. When a college student has an adulterous affair, there will be negative consequences for sure, but when a pastor of a vibrant church has an affair, the negative impact is more far-reaching and affects more lives. There is greater collateral damage; the painful penalty and impact of the sin is greater.

"Yeah, but what about grace and restoration?" Because of grace we can confess our sin and turn from what we know is wrong. We can be restored to fellowship and right relationship with God, but there may still be consequences for our sin. Resuming a position with the same level of authority may never happen. If restoration is to happen, it should be a gradual regaining of trust. If a babysitter beats one of my children black and blue, she will probably never babysit my children again. I don't care how sincere the repentance and apology are, she severely abused a great trust. Trust is a hard thing to regain and will take time. Forgiveness is different than trust. I can forgive a person and still not trust him/her. Forgiveness is a first step in rebuilding trust, but depending on the injury, full trust may never be achieved.

I'm not trying to be brutal, harsh or vindictive; I'm trying to put the fear of God in you. Do not be deceived. Don't listen to those abusers of God's grace who play with fire and act as if there will never be any consequences to sin. If God tells you to not play in the street or you will be road pizza, and then you are seen dancing on the highway saying, "Look at me! Look at me! Haha, I'm not road pizza!" don't deceive yourself into thinking that you can dodge semi-trucks forever. If you can't do the time, then don't do the crime.

> *Now all these things happened to them as examples,*
> *and they were written for our admonition, upon whom*
> *the ends of the ages have come.*
> *— 1 Corinthians 10:11*

> *It happened in the spring of the year, at the time when kings*
> *go out to battle, that David sent Joab and his servants with*
> *him, and all Israel; and they destroyed the people*
> *of Ammon and besieged Rabbah. But David remained at*
> *Jerusalem. Then it happened one evening that David*
> *rose from his bed and walked on the roof of the king's house.*
> *And from the roof he saw a woman bathing, and the*
> *woman was very beautiful to behold. So David sent and*
> *nquired about the woman. And someone said, "Is this not*
> *Bathsheba, the daughter of Eliam, the wife of Uriah the*
> *Hittite?" Then David sent messengers, and took her; and*
> *she came to him, and he lay with her, for she was cleansed*
> *from her impurity; and she returned to her house.*
> *And the woman conceived; so she sent and told David,*
> *and said, "I am with child."*
> *— 2 Samuel 11:1-5*

I have some observations and thoughts about this passage in 2 Samuel. The first somewhat obvious thing is that King David was shirking his responsibilities by not going to war. This was David's main calling; he was like Joshua in that he was a military general, a man of war. David was a warrior poet, called to conquer and secure the Promised Land for the people of God. Solomon was called to something totally different.

He was called to a time of peace and building the majestic temple; the name Solomon means "peaceful." The peaceful and prosperous reign of King Solomon could not have been possible if he had not been preceded by the warrior reign of King David. It is important to know your calling and stay in your calling. If you are called to pastor a church and you decide it's too hard so you quit, you are making yourself vulnerable to sin. You may think you're making your life easier by avoiding hardship, but you may just be jumping from the frying pan into the fire. It's important to pray through important decisions and uncover the mind of God on your situation. Making huge decisions when you are emotionally low or high is not wise.

We can't read David's mind as to why he was shirking his duty and not going off to war. The scriptures don't always tell us everything we want to know, just everything we need to know to live successful, godly lives (see 2 Peter 1:2-4). I do know human nature though, and King David is not much different from you and me. David might have been thinking, "I need some ME time. I need to reward myself. I've worked so hard crushing my enemies under my feet and grinding them to dust. Yeah, I think I'll go up on the roof of my palace and check out the local babes." Some folks are always whining about how hard they work and they seem to take a sabbatical every month. They are always slipping away for some ME time. I am not against vacations and I'm not advocating a workaholic lifestyle, but there is an ol' saying, "Idle hands are the devil's workshop." Just hanging around trying to invent ways of entertaining yourself can get old fast. If you are continually trying to avoid what you're supposed to be doing, you are going to find yourself in trouble.

The other part of the story that bugs me is that Bathsheba was sponge bathing in full view of the palace roof. Is it possible that she wanted to be seen? Is it possible she was crushing on David and saw an opportunity to be upwardly-mobile? Why be the wife of a Mighty Man when you can be Queen? Any honorable woman would not visit a man late at night when her husband is away. The Bible doesn't record that she put up a fight. There is a lesson here for women as well: be careful how you're advertising. You just may get what you want. Bathsheba suffered here as well. Her husband Uriah was killed in battle (ordered to a hot spot by King David), and her firstborn baby died. These things had to leave a scar. Please don't take me wrong here, the man is almost always more to blame than the woman. That's the price of leadership; the leader is always more accountable. In the Garden of Eden, it was Adam that God confronted first. Why? Because he was the guy in charge. A man cannot date rape a woman and claim it was the woman's fault. No matter how seductive the woman is, the man is held to a higher standard and accountability. On the other hand, women of God must learn to walk in wisdom. Not all men are honorable. A woman should not be out alone late at night without a chaperone; you can call me old fashioned, or just call it good sense.

SOLOMON AND HIS WIVES

In those days I also saw Jews who had married women of Ashdod, Ammon, and Moab. And half of their children spoke the language of Ashdod, and could not speak the language of Judah, but spoke according to the language of one or the other people.

So I contended with them and cursed them, struck some of them and pulled out their hair, and made them swear by God, saying, "You shall not give your daughters as wives to their sons, nor take their daughters for your sons or yourselves. Did not Solomon king of Israel sin by these things? Yet among many nations there was no king like him, who was beloved of his God; and God made him king over all Israel. Nevertheless pagan women caused even him to sin. Should we then hear of your doing all this great evil, transgressing against our God by marrying pagan women?"
— Nehemiah 13:23-27

But King Solomon loved many foreign women, as well as the daughter of Pharaoh: women of the Moabites, Ammonites, Edomites, Sidonians, and Hittites — from the nations of whom the LORD had said to the children of Israel, "You shall not intermarry with them, nor they with you. Surely they will turn away your hearts after their gods." Solomon clung to these in love. And he had seven hundred wives, princesses, and three hundred concubines; and his wives turned away his heart.
— 1 Kings 11:1-3

(Please read 1 Kings, chapter 11, in its entirety)

There is a lesson here for New Testament Christians but you have to track with me. God foresaw that Israel would have kings so He had Moses write down some ground rules for them (see Deuteronomy 17:14-20). There were three simple rules: don't multiply gold, horses or wives. Solomon in his unbridled greed and lust set world records in all three categories. I mean come on… a thousand wives?!? This is a serious lust problem.

The Old Testament allowed multiple wives. Some things are allowed but not always the best for us. Families with multiple wives always had problems with jealousy and infighting. On the upside, multiple wives did help with a more rapid growth in population in a brutal war-torn age. Also, after the flood of Noah, it helped to re-populate the earth. One thing to note is that in the beginning, God created one man and one woman as a family model. Although God permitted it in the Old Testament, the New Testament commands only one wife (see 1 Timothy 3:2).

It wasn't wrong for Solomon to marry foreign women, it was wrong to marry foreign women who would not convert to Judaism. The command by God not to marry foreign women was not racist. God was concerned with maintaining the purity of Yahweh worship, not the purity of race. If someone from another race converted to the Jewish religion, they could intermarry with God's people. Such was the case of Ruth the Moabite marrying Boaz and becoming part of the genealogy of King David and the Christ. Moses married an Ethiopian woman and brought criticism from his racist brother and sister, but God was not upset. As long as the person is a true worshiper of the God of Abraham, Isaac, and Jacob, it's not a problem.

This brings me to our lesson for Christians of our time and age. The command to not intermarry with people of other religions is still in effect for believers in Christ.

> *A wife is bound by law as long as her husband lives; but if her husband dies, she is at liberty to be married to whom she wishes, only in the Lord.*
> *— 1 Corinthians 7:39*

> *Do not be unequally yoked together with unbelievers. For what fellowship has righteousness with lawlessness? And what communion has light with darkness? And what*

> *accord has Christ with Belial? Or what part has a believer with an unbeliever? And what agreement has the temple of God with idols? For you are the temple of the living God.*
> *— 2 Corinthians 6:14-16a*

If God in His wisdom and foresight has determined that having a romantic relationship with an unbeliever can at the least cause you to go through a lot of hurt, and at worst influence you to compromise your faith in Christ, then who are you to argue? You will always be able to find people to help you justify sin. Not everyone respects God and His Word. *"There is no wisdom or understanding or counsel against the Lord" (Proverbs 21:30).* King Solomon had great wisdom and even he was led astray by pagan women. You are not smarter than Solomon, and you and I are definitely not wiser than God and His Word. You are in control of your heart and have a responsibility to guard it with all diligence.

> *Above all else, guard your heart, for it is the wellspring of life*
> *— Proverbs 4:23 NIV*

RECAP

Let's recap this chapter and reinforce the lessons the Word of God teaches. If you are wise you will listen to the Lord and guard your heart against sexual lust. You **cannot** out-flank the penalty for sin. You **can** receive God's infinite grace and yield to the power of self-control made available through the Holy Spirit.

- Defend the high ground of the eye gate and the heart gate. Keep your eyes from evil and guard your emotional attachments.

- Samson and Delilah: If you keep messing with sexual sin, you're going to eventually fall hard.
- Joseph and Potiphar's wife: Don't put yourself in compromising situations, great reward and promotion come to those who keep themselves pure.
- David and Bathsheba: Idle hands are the devil's workshop.
- Solomon and his wives: As Christians, we should keep ourselves from romantic relationships with those who do not share our faith.

*Parenting is a tricky thing.
There is no such thing as
a perfect parent or a perfect child.
We do the best we can do.*

Chapter 10

Good Parenting Brings Promotion

When my wife and daughters shop at the mall, I sometimes go along. Shopping for clothes is not my favorite sport, but hey, I get to spend time with the family. When they go into a girly store to try on clothes, I get very uncomfortable. Therefore, I elect to sit out in the mall on a comfortable leather chair and "people watch." Now, *this* is a fascinating sport. I get out my smartphone and start reading an on-line book and occasionally glance up when disturbed by the cacophony of sounds from an endless parade of humanity. It's amazing how diverse humankind is; different shapes, sizes, ages, and clothing styles. As people pass by, I try to imagine their life and I make up fictitious storylines in my mind. Once I saw a distinguished older man, sharply dressed, who seemed to be looking and waiting for someone. Looking into his eyes, I could see a tenderness and brokenness. Perhaps he's a widower and is meeting up with his high school sweetheart, you know, the one that got away? He is anxious and wondering if the flame is still there.

As I sit and watch, I observe all kinds of scenarios. Young girls in their early teenage years whispering and giggling (some things never change). Cool guys strutting by who have made "cool" a terminal disease. Then there is a young mother pushing a stroller followed by two preschoolers. There is a little play area in the center of the mall, so I'm sure they had just come from there. It was so cute watching the little boy and girl walk behind mom like ducklings. I thought to myself, that is a good mom. When you are a young parent and have three young children in tow, you don't have much money and often feel trapped in the house. What a good plan; walk around the mall, let the kids get some energy out and you don't have to spend any money.

Parenting is a tricky thing. There is no such thing as a perfect parent or a perfect child. We do the best we can. The Bible gives us wisdom and principles, but no child comes with an individualized owner's manual, tailor-made to the child's specific disposition. Wouldn't it be great if there were little instruction tags that came with each child? They would probably say something like –

Child #1 owner's manual: The child you have just received is a high spirited young man and will take a strong hand. Being intelligent also, you will need eyes in the back of your head. There will be no need for you to have a personal diet plan during the first ten years of this child's life, for you will need all of your waking energy to keep up with him. If you keep on him and help him to be disciplined and focused, he will become a great leader.

Child #2 owner's manual: The child you have just received is a sensitive little girl. You will hardly have to raise your voice to her because she is eager to please. She has a very creative and active mind and will play for hours by herself. Being introverted, she will need to be pushed into social interaction. If you are nurturing and sensitive to her, she will become a scientist or a novelist.

Unfortunately, each child does not come with an instruction label. We are left with seeking God and trying our best to apply the principles of the Bible. When I left the hospital with my firstborn, I was petrified. I couldn't believe they would let me walk out of there with this innocent, delicate child. They didn't know me from Adam. How could they, or God for that matter, trust me with this responsibility? The weight of it all seemed so overwhelming.

YOUR DESTINY IS CONNECTED WITH YOUR CHILDREN

> *And the LORD said, "Shall I hide from Abraham what I am doing, since Abraham shall surely become a great and mighty nation, and all the nations of the earth shall be blessed in him? For I have known him, in order **that he may command his children and his household after him, that they keep the way of the LORD, to do righteousness and justice, that the LORD may bring to Abraham what He has spoken to him.**"*
> — Genesis 18:17-19

For God to bring to Abraham what He had promised, Abraham had to be successful in commanding his children in the ways of the Lord; *"that the Lord may bring to pass what He has spoken to Abraham."* Our destiny in God and life-time achievement is connected with how we raise our children and whether they follow God's plan for their life. If we fail the test of parenting, then our fruitfulness and success will be diminished. Have you known leaders in the kingdom whose children became so rancid that it affected their ministry? The load of ministry is taxing enough, but add to that the emotional and financial cost of the sins of the children, and it can be overwhelming. This is why stipulations were made in the Bible concerning the qualifications of spiritual leadership.

> *One who rules his own house well, having his children in submission with all reverence. For if a man does not know how to rule his own house, how will he take care of the church of God?*
> *— 1 Timothy 3:4-5*

There truly is a direct correlation between the way a man (or woman) parents and the style of leadership they will employ in the church. If they are dominating, bullying and smothering at home, they will be that way in the church. If they are too passive and non-confrontive at home, then their leadership will reflect that imbalance. We are being tested and prepared for promotion - or demotion through our home life and parenting skills.

Don't throw this book across the room in frustration and hopeless condemnation. Track with me through this chapter and I believe the Lord will give insight and wisdom to turn things around if you're on the wrong track. There are some situations where even if you do everything right, the child will rebel for a season. God Himself is a perfect parent, and yet from the Garden of Eden on, He had children who rebelled (see Isaiah 30:1). When there is one child in the family who strays it can be excused away, but when all the children have rebelled against the ways of God, then we may have a problem. And the problem may be with bad parenting. Please read this entire chapter. Fulfilling your God-given call and the eternal destiny of your children are at stake.

GOD THINKS GENERATIONALLY

Then the LORD appeared to Abram and said, "To your descendants I will give this land." And there he built an altar to the LORD, who had appeared to him.
— Genesis 12:7

One generation shall praise Your works to another, And shall declare Your mighty acts.
— Psalm 145:4

When all that generation had been gathered to their fathers, another generation arose after them who did not know the LORD nor the work which He had done for Israel. Then the children of Israel did evil in the sight of the LORD, and served the Baals.
— Judges 2:10-11

When God sees you, He sees all the generations after you. We as Christians have to think like God. We have to prioritize ministry to the next generation. Adult ministry will always be important because when you have spiritually healthy adults you will have healthy children. but we need to be majorly investing into Children and Youth ministry. We are always just one generation away from losing tremendous ground in the Spirit and being a morally bankrupt nation.

There was a king in the Bible whose name was Hezekiah. In a moment of weakness, he showed ambassadors from the Kingdom of Babylon all the riches of his house and capital city of Jerusalem. The prophet Isaiah was sent by God to admonish him for his pride.

Then Isaiah said to Hezekiah, "Hear the word of the LORD of hosts: 'Behold, the days are coming when all that is in your

> *house, and what your fathers have accumulated until this day, shall be carried to Babylon; nothing shall be left,' says the LORD. 'And they shall take away some of your sons who will descend from you, whom you will beget; and they shall be eunuchs in the palace of the king of Babylon.'" So Hezekiah said to Isaiah, "The word of the LORD which you have spoken is good!" For he said, "At least there will be peace and truth in my days."*
> — Isaiah 39:5-8

After receiving such a grievous prophetic word, King Hezekiah didn't tear into his clothes, he didn't fast and weep before the Lord, he didn't even attempt to cry out to God and try to get Him to change His mind. He simply said, "The word is good! At least there will be peace in my days." He was completely unconcerned with the evil that would befall the next generation. A chapter earlier he was dying of a tumorous growth and he cried out for mercy and God miraculously healed him! This time, when disaster is pronounced on the next generation, he is indifferent and apathetic! Let this not be said of us.

I've seen parents go through terrible spiritual attacks and the ultimate target was the children. The enemy of our souls is unrelenting in going after the next generation. He knows that if he can get the children, he can turn a nation. He knows that if he can take your children out, he can diminish your impact for the Kingdom of God. The main responsibility that we have as Christian parents is to train our children in the ways of God.

> *And these words which I command you today shall be in your heart. You shall teach them diligently to your children, and shall talk of them when you sit in your house, when you walk by the way, when you lie down, and when you rise up.*
> — Deuteronomy 6:6-7

The above verse is not just about having devotionals with your children, it's about you and your life being a living devotional. When God holds first place in your life and you are doing the best you can to live your faith in the open, your children cannot help but be greatly impacted.

When I was very young, my family would go to Grandpa and Grandma's house in hilly northern Michigan. My grandpa's older sister lived with them, and we affectionately called her "Little Grandma" because she was only about 4 feet 9 inches tall. She would sometimes play with us and had a very infectious laugh. At night, before I went upstairs to bed, I would knock softly on her bedroom door. Her loving voice would say, "Come on in, Alan Junior." I would find her sitting up in bed, a pillow behind her back, nestled under the blankets with a Bible on her lap. I would ask, "Little Grandma, what are you reading?" Her response was, "I'm reading God's book. I always put the Word of God in my heart before I go to sleep." That was all she said. She never preached at me or tried to force a lesson upon me. She was the Bible lesson. The example of such a wonderful person reading her Bible every night before bed had a lasting impact on me.

THE EXTREMES OF PARENTING

A false balance is abomination to the LORD:
but a just weight is his delight.
— Proverbs 11:1 KJV

When I teach the principles of scripture, I like to show extremes. By showing the polar opposites of an issue we can clearly see the imbalances. There is a ditch on both sides of the road; somewhere in the middle is the balance. When things are too extreme and out of balance, they are an abomination to the Lord. I realize that the above verse is concerned with not cheating people in the marketplace, but applying the verse to the imbalanced perspectives of life is a sound application. When there are extremes, people get cheated out of many blessings.

In parenting, two extremes will invariably cause children to rebel and be resentful of authority. The first is a **passive parent** who is too permissive. The second is a **despot parent** who is dominating, bullying style that smothers. Let me expound on these.

The Passive Parent:

> *The rod and rebuke give wisdom,*
> *But a child left to himself brings shame to his mother.*
> *— Proverbs 29:15*

Children do not raise themselves well. You can't let children make all of their own decisions and expect them to figure it out. Children need guidance and boundaries to make them feel secure and develop into confident adults. They need mentors.

One philosophy of parenting I never agreed with in a Christian home is giving children a choice to serve Christ and go to church. My children never had a choice. I told them that when they are out on their own, then they can choose not to serve the living God, but "While you are in this house and under this roof, you will live by my rules. We are a church-going family and you will attend church with us at least twice a week. It's my job as your parent to lead you in positive habits that will lead to a highly successful life." God told Abraham that He knew him, "*...in order that he may* **command his**

children *and his household after him, that they keep the way of the LORD..." (see Genesis 18:19).*

I've heard all the arguments against my parenting stance. Some say, "By shoving church down their throat and forcing them to go, it will turn them off to church. That's the reason I'm not a Christian; my parents forced me to go to church." First of all, this is a lame excuse for not serving Christ. You'll be standing before the judgment and Jesus will say, "Why didn't you serve Me? I had a great plan for your life." This is how your lame excuse will sound, "It's my parents' fault. If they hadn't made me go to church twice a week I might have chosen to serve You on my own. But noooo, they shoved religion down my throat." Does this sound like it will hold up before God Almighty? I can just hear how Jesus will respond, "Let Me ask you something. Were you forced to go to school growing up? And yet, you continued with education after high school. Were you forced to brush your teeth and practice good hygiene? And yet, for the rest of your life, you took good care of yourself physically. You brushed your teeth, shaved regularly and bathed. Being lovingly disciplined with good life habits is a good thing. You made a moral choice of your own volition to turn away from the God of your youth."

Your children need to respect you before they can be your bud. As your child grows and develops, there will be a natural change in the dynamics of your relationship. When they are toddlers, you can't give long explanations for saying no. When they become teenagers and announce their emancipation from all restraint, you must be prepared to use all the leverage at your disposal to corral them. They need to know that you are strong enough to secure the borders. A happy and secure child has consistent boundaries. When they have submitted to discipline, eventually they will become self-disciplined. The life habits that you reinforce will stay with them. When they go off on their own, then you can have a wonderful friendship with your adult children. They will respect you enough to seek your advice.

Please don't get me wrong. I am not saying that our relationship with our children should always be as the "long arm of the law." Rules without relationship will breed rebellion, but being too passive and giving little Johnny and Susie everything they want will bring destruction on them as well.

Let me ask you a question. Who makes the spiritual decisions in your home? Who decides what church you will attend as a family? Do you, or your children? It's not wrong to get some input from your kids, but you, as the parent, are the one to make the final call. Your kids need to learn to submit to your decisions. Authority in life is not always going to take a poll to find out where the political winds are blowing. God Himself does not always ask my opinion. How we teach our children to submit to authority is a very important life skill. It will determine how they submit to God's authority.

I was the chaplain for a Christian school and there was a problem with one of the kindergarteners. Every time the boy was given a directive, he would scream and hide under his desk. The mother had to be called in for a meeting with me and the teacher. The mother said, "I don't understand this. He never gives me problems like this at home." I responded with the question, "Do you ever tell your child no at home? Because you're too passive with this child at home, he doesn't know how to respond to authority he doesn't agree with." In time, the boy adapted to the boundaries and rules at school. When we give in too often to whining children, they are shocked when all authority does not bend to their fits and whine.

The priest Eli is a good example of passive parenting in the Bible. He would warn his sons with words but he never followed up with action. He was rebuked for not restraining his children and it led to their death (see 1 Samuel 2:12-36, 3:11-14, 4:11).

The Despot Parent:

(Please read 1 Kings 12:1-24)

In the above Bible story, we see a king that had too heavy of hand and it led to rebellion. This is the polar opposite of the Passive Parent. God didn't give us children so we could be on a power surge, having some Napoleon complex where our children are the only people we can boss around and it somehow makes us feel empowered in some perverse way. Let me repeat a principle I said earlier: *rules without relationship will breed rebellion*. We are servant leaders in the home as well as the workplace. Yes, we are to be the established leader in the home, but to be too smothering, dominating and oppressive is an extreme that will lead your children down a path of resentment for authority.

I must say as a pastor, I've seen the extreme of "Passive Parenting" more than the "Despot Parent." Many parents allow false guilt to overwhelm them and they become too ingratiating, but there is a ditch on both sides of the road, and the opposite extreme of being too passive is being despotic.

> *And they spoke to him, saying, "If you will be a servant to these people today, and serve them, and answer them, and speak good words to them, then they will be your servants forever."*
> — 1 Kings 12:7

Another aspect of being too oppressive is found in the words we speak over our children. Constant negative words are very damaging to sensitive spirits who need affirmation and encouragement. Instead of saying things like, "You idiot," "You're so clumsy," "You break everything you touch," "Why do you never listen?", try rephrasing your words to address the problem, and yet be more affirming. "What can we learn from that mistake? You are so smart I know you will do better," "You're so beautiful and graceful but you shouldn't have been playing that way in the house. You need to apologize and we will find a way to make this right." It is possible to be affirming and still hold them responsible for their actions. It's possible to make a distinction between the negative action and the identity of the child.

> *Pleasant words are like a honeycomb,*
> *Sweetness to the soul and health to the bones.*
> — Proverbs 16:24

If our whole relationship with our children is correcting them all the time, then we have a problem. This pattern started to happen to me with one of my kids, and it was greatly grieving me. I sought the Lord about this and I felt a witness in my spirit that I should begin praising my child whenever she did even the slightest thing well. Besides negative consequences for bad behavior, there should also be a reward for doing well. If the child is only getting attention for bad behavior, then we are inadvertently reinforcing negative actions and thinking.

I'm not saying it's easy to turn the ship around. You may have to look hard to find things to compliment but God will help you.

These are the two styles of parenting that are too extreme. If we are overly smothering with correction, we will create sneaky liars. They will have a fierce aversion to all authority and may become criminal masterminds. If we are too permissive, we will create willful, undisciplined barbarians. Somewhere in the middle is the balance. Look for good mentors. If you admire the good job someone has done in raising their children, befriend them; they can be a treasure of helpful advice.

WHAT TO DO WHEN CHILDREN STRAY

Thus says the LORD:
"Refrain your voice from weeping,
And your eyes from tears;
For your work shall be rewarded, says the LORD,
And they shall come back from the land of the enemy.
There is hope in your future, says the LORD,
That your children shall come back to their own border."
— Jeremiah 31:16-17

This is a great promise to parents who have lost children to the world. Our hope is in three things: **The promises of God, the power of the seed of God's Word planted in their heart, and the power of our prayers.**

When I pray for wayward children, I pray along these lines:

- Lord, let the Word of God planted in their heart speak to them; let it rise up in their spirit and convict them (see Proverbs 6:22-23, Isaiah 55:10-11).

- Send faithful witnesses to them who will talk to them about Jesus (see Matthew 9:38).
- Have mercy, O God, and bring them to the end of themselves. Bring them to a place where their only hope is in You. Grant them repentance to the acknowledging of the truth (see 2 Timothy 2:25-26).

> But when he came to himself, he said, "How many of my father's hired servants have bread enough and to spare, and I perish with hunger! I will arise and go to my father, and will say to him, 'Father, I have sinned against heaven and before you, and I am no longer worthy to be called your son. Make me like one of your hired servants.'"
> — Luke 15:17-19

(Please read the story of the Prodigal Son – Luke 15:11-32)

The parable of the Prodigal Son brings great hope. We not only see a wayward person coming to their end, but we see a loving father longing for his return. When the son came to himself and returned home, his father didn't rub his face in his failure. God had worked on the prodigal and brought him to a true and full repentance. When the son returned, he was brought to full restoration.

You can be a great parent and still have a child rebel. In the story of the Prodigal Son, the father's home was in order. The reason the rebellious son had to leave home was because he was not allowed to live in an unwholesome way while under his father's roof. The father also allowed the son, whom he loved, to reach his bottom and come to repentance. Sometimes we shelter our kids, pay for their sins, and enable their prodigal lifestyle.

A distraught mother came to me, begging me to pray that her son would not go to jail. Her son was a drunken bum. He was finally pulled over for drunk driving and put in jail. The mother was more concerned about jail being on his record than the potential danger he posed on the road while driving drunk. I, for one, was glad he was in jail, and for the life of me I couldn't understand how he escaped serving time for several years. I reassured her that Jesus is in the jail with her son. I refused to pray that he would avoid a long period of service in the county jail, but instead prayed that he would sober up, come to his end, and consider his life. After a month in jail, he requested to see me, and I had a wonderful chance to lead him to Christ. Praise the Lord.

I'm not saying that we should not help our children who are in trouble. I am saying that we should pray for God's wisdom to discern when we are enabling their rebellion or not. Allowing them to come to their end must happen for them to be restored to a right relationship with you and their heavenly Father.

CHILDREN NEED MORE THAN INFORMATION, THEY NEED GOD ENCOUNTERS

When children leave home or go to college, they are challenged for the first time as to whether they are going to follow through with their faith. Why is it that so many of our young people leave the faith when they get out from under the authority of Mom and Dad? I mean, these kids have been steeped in all the Bible stories, they have been through Bible quiz programs where they memorize vast amounts of facts and scripture verses, and yet after pouring data about God, church and the Bible into them, they walk away.

The answer, my friend, is that *an experience is worth a thousand arguments*. A child that experiences powerful God encounters will seldom stray. Information about God is one thing, knowing Him personally is something else entirely. Jesus said, *"And this is eternal life, that they may know You, the only true God, and Jesus Christ whom You have sent." (John 17:3-4)*. Possessing eternal life itself is based on knowing God personally, not just knowing about Him.

> *Now the sons of Eli were corrupt; they did not know the LORD.*
> *— 1 Samuel 2:12*

I have a problem with this verse. Here are two young men who were raised in the things of God. They were PKs (Preacher's Kids). They were mentored in the family trade, which was the priesthood. They knew the Pentateuch (the five books of Moses) by memory. They not only knew the law of Moses, but they knew all the ceremonial rituals and sacrifices as well. How could someone be around this much God stuff and never know God?

The word for "know" in the above passage is the Hebrew word "yada." It means to know intimately, to recognize, to acknowledge, to be acquainted with. In some instances, it means to know sexually, "Now Adam knew Eve his wife, and she conceived..." (see Genesis 4:1). With all the training that Eli's boys had in church, they never had a God encounter. They never met God in a personal way.

> *Now Samuel did not yet know the LORD: The word of the LORD had not yet been revealed to him. The LORD called Samuel third time, and Samuel got up and went to Eli and said, "Here I am; you called me."*
> *— 1 Samuel 3:7-8 NIV*

The same pattern was happening in the training of Samuel. In learning all the duties of a priest, he was charged with keeping the candelabra lit in the Tabernacle. One night God introduced Himself to him in a powerful encounter. The contrast between the prophet/priest Samuel and the two sons of Eli could not be more profound. Samuel knew God and encountered Him intimately and became one of Israel's most renowned and powerful prophets.

The obvious question poses itself: How do I position my children to have powerful God-encounters so that they know God personally? I am so glad you asked. What I am about to say is from a Charismatic/Pentecostal perspective so if you're not into the fullness of the Spirit, then I don't know what to tell you. This is what I know, and this is what I teach.

- In Children's Church, make sure they are having prayer times at the end of class where kids can examine their hearts and repent for things the Holy Spirit is convicting them of. This will keep them tender.
- Train them to pray for the sick and others at church and in class. When God answers their prayers, it will have a huge impact on their faith.
- Children should be trained in hearing from God as well. Prayer journals are great. You should set aside some time in class, and at home, for them to write down something they feel God is saying to them. Parents: Share with your children how you discern God's voice. You will be astounded at what happens next! What they share with you will blow your mind!
- After a good teaching on the Baptism in the Holy Spirit (see Matthew 3:11, Acts 1:5, 2:4, 10:44-48),

explain that the Holy Spirit must be received by those who want Him. Lay hands on them to receive.
- Encourage those who are baptized in the Holy Spirit to use their prayer language daily. Encourage them to pray in the Spirit during the prayer times (see Jude 20, 1 Corinthians 14:15, 39).
- Church camp is a great place to have life-altering God encounters. Many missionaries and preachers received their call to ministry at a church camp.
- When your children have a need, pray with them and expect God to answer. When the answer comes, point it out to your children and watch their faith grow.

Let's wrap up what we have learned in this chapter:
- Our children did not come with a manual. We must pray for God's wisdom with each child and utilize clear child-rearing principles.
- Your destiny is connected with your children. God thinks generationally; our potential is diminished when our children fail to follow God's plan for their lives. The opposite is also true; if our children follow Christ, then our potential is enhanced.
- Our house may be in proper order and yet a child may choose to walk away from God, but when the majority, or all, of our children are not serving God, then the problem is parenting.
- If your children are not serving God wholeheartedly, there are ways to pray for them. Time to go to war. It's never too late for God to change lives.
- We must avoid the extremes of parenting; do not be overly permissive or overly dominating. Rules without relationship will breed rebellion. God

doesn't just give us rules, He gives us relationship, and because of that relationship, we want to obey the rules.

- Information about God is not enough; our children need to be positioned to have God encounters. Only by knowing God personally can we be born again.

The Lord repay your work, and a full reward be given you by the Lord God of Israel, under whose wings you have come for refuge.
Ruth 2:12

Chapter 11

Look to the Reward

THE REWARD IS REAL

*But without faith it is impossible to please Him, for he who comes to God must believe that He is, and that **He is a rewarder** of those who diligently seek Him.*
— Hebrews 11:6

This Bible verse is probably the most well-known among Christians concerning reward. Consider what God is saying here, that it pleases Him that we look to the reward. This is part of our faith walk, to not only believe that God exists but to believe that He rewards the diligent. It's impossible for God to lie so if He promises reward, the reward is real (see Titus 1:2).

What does God's reward look like? When we peruse through the Bible from cover to cover, we see a myriad of rewards. In the case of Abraham, some of the promised reward was to be realized by the generations following. Some rewards are for this life, some are for our descendants, and some extend into eternity.

One of my favorite Bible stories is that of Ruth, a Moabite widow who left her people to take care of her mother-in-law and serve the God of Israel. She became one of only two women who were mentioned in the genealogy of Christ (see Matthew 1:5). Amazingly, both women were foreigners who converted to Judaism. They became foreshadows and types of the Gentile nations coming to Christ by faith and being partakers of the great promises and rewards.

I love what Boaz pronounces over Ruth:

> *"The LORD repay your work, and **a full reward** be given you by the LORD God of Israel, under whose wings you have come for refuge."*
> *— Ruth 2:12*

If we are honest, we have to admit there have been times when we believed God with all our heart and things didn't turn out so well. God didn't fit into our neat little box. We looked to the reward and felt let down and cheated. What we believed didn't match the outcome, and we were left in crisis mode. The psychological term for this experience is called "cognitive dissonance." It is the result of incongruous beliefs. When something happens that doesn't jibe with our belief system, we can go into a tailspin.

Years ago a young couple in my church were believing to get pregnant. When she finally became pregnant, a few months into her pregnancy the doctors gave her some bad news. She was told that the child in the womb was badly deformed and that an abortion would be an option. If the baby was brought to term, it probably would not live long outside the womb. This couple did not believe that an abortion was the right thing to do. They confided in my wife and I, and we agreed in prayer for a miracle. After the baby girl was born, she lived only a few short hours and died. It was very heartbreaking. As I was making funeral arrangements with the father, we got into one of those "Why did God allow this?" discussions. Unanswerable questions and insoluble experiences are the hallmark of Cognitive Dissonance.

It was at this time that I perceived something profound from the Holy Spirit. I knew it was from the Holy Spirit because I am not that wise on my own. I shared with my friend, who had just lost his baby that trust when we don't understand is the highest form of faith. Our faith may fail us, but trust in the Lord when we don't understand will never fail us.

> *Trust in the LORD with all your heart, and lean not on your own understanding; In all your ways acknowledge Him, and He shall direct your paths.*
> *— Proverbs 3:5-6*

> *The secret things belong to the LORD our God, but those things which are revealed belong to us and to our children forever, that we may do all the words of this law.*
> *— Deuteronomy 29:29*

There will always be things that we do not understand; unanswerable questions. In those seasons our faith must rise to the level of trust. Bitterness toward God will erode our faith and cheat us of a reward. We are encouraged in the epistle of Colossians to not let false beliefs and wrong thinking creep in and rob us of good things to come. *"Let no one cheat you of your reward"* (Colossians 2:18).

In a fallen, sinful world where evil things happen, we must trust in the ultimate goodness of God and look forward to that goodness. Oral Roberts used to say, "God is a good God and the devil is a bad devil."

> *I would have lost heart, unless I had believed*
> *That I would see the goodness of the LORD*
> *In the land of the living.*
> — Psalm 27:13

Although the rewards of serving the living God are vast and opulent, the greatest reward is God Himself! When you have God, you have it all! This is what God told Abraham:

> *After these things the word of the LORD came to Abram in a vision, saying, "Do not be afraid, Abram. I am your shield, your exceedingly great reward."*
> — Genesis 15:1

The Word of God promises us many rewards but having a friendship with the creator of the universe is the ultimate reward. Jesus said that knowing God personally is the gateway to eternal life. Ask Jesus to be your personal Lord and Savior and begin enjoying the greatest reward, God Himself.

> *And this is eternal life, that they may know You, the only true God, and Jesus Christ whom You have sent.*
> — John 17:3

MOSES LOOKED TO THE REWARD

> *By faith Moses, when he became of age, refused to be called the son of Pharaoh's daughter, choosing rather to suffer affliction with the people of God than to enjoy the passing pleasures of sin, esteeming the reproach of Christ greater riches than the treasures in Egypt; for he looked to the reward. By faith he forsook Egypt, not fearing the wrath of the king; for he endured as seeing Him who is invisible.*
> — Hebrews 11:24-27

Moses looked to the reward of obedience and to his relationship with God almighty. Maintaining his friendship with Yahweh was more important than anything. What was the reward that Moses looked to? What could possibly be a greater reward than a life of privilege and power as a prince of Egypt? There is a fleeting comfort of fame and fortune offered by this life that has distracted many from fulfilling great things for the Kingdom of God. Moses gave up temporary glory for eternal glory as one of THE most influential human beings of all time. Following God's call dwarfed anything Moses could have done. As a prince of Egypt, he would have just been a hardly noticed footnote in history. Instead, by following God he changed the world. When we get to heaven, we will discover the immense impact of people whose lives were hardly noticed while they passed through this world.

There was the rich young ruler that went away from Jesus very sorrowful because he didn't want to leave his comfort and become a personal disciple of Jesus (see Matthew 19:16-22). Think of what Jesus was offering him; Jesus was asking him to be one of the twelve Apostles of the lamb! In the future Kingdom, at the second coming of Christ, he would have ruled one of the tribes of Israel (see Matthew 19:28-30)! The rich young ruler chose the temporary comfort of this life over helping Jesus change the lives of countless generations by spreading the Gospel of peace and forgiveness.

In the parable of the Sower, Jesus taught that there are four different kinds of ground on which the seed of God's Word falls: 1) the hard path, 2) stony ground with shallow soil, 3) ground filled with thorns, and 4) good ground that bears 30, 60, and 100 fold (see Matthew 13:18-23). The thorny ground is people who never come to a place of mega fruitfulness because they looked more to the temporary comfort and the reward of this life rather than living sacrificially for Christ.

> *Now he who received seed among the thorns is he who hears the word, and the cares of this world and the deceitfulness of riches choke the word, and he becomes unfruitful.*
> *— Matthew 13:22*

How many potentially great ministers of the Gospel have been lost to the cares of this world and the deceitfulness of riches? There is an analogy of a monkey with his hand in a cookie jar. The hunter nails a jar to a tree with a cookie inside. The monkey comes along and reaches into the jar, grabs the cookie, and then can't pull his hand out again. The opening of the jar is only large enough for the monkey's hand. While the monkey is grasping the cookie, he can't pull his hand out, and the hunter walks up to the monkey and whacks him over the head. The monkey could have escaped at any time, but he didn't want to let go of the cookie. Is there something you are holding onto that is keeping you from following the call of God?

Giving up the illusion of material comfort for the call of God takes some moxie faith. God has promised an abundant provision to those who seek Him first. Everything you need to fulfill the call of God is yours when you put God and His kingdom first. A worry-free, abundant supply is one of the rewards.

> *But seek first the kingdom of God and His righteousness, and all these things shall be added to you.*
> *— Matthew 6:33*

*And God is able to make all grace abound toward you,
that you, always having all sufficiency in all things,
may have an abundance for every good work.*
— *2 Corinthians 9:8*

One of the hardest things I had to walk away from was some toxic friends. Our friendships were based on a lot of alcohol and Rock-n-Roll. The party lifestyle and playing music was what I lived for. I had to break their influence over me before I could influence them with the Gospel. One night, after I became a Born Again Christian, a group of friends picked me up to go partying. I brought this big black Bible into the car and there was this uncomfortable silence. Finally, the driver speaks up and says, "Why are you bringing that big Bible?"

I responded, "You guys said this was a BYOB party, right? Bring Your Own Bible?"

"NO! That was Bring Your Own Beer."

"Oh man, my bad. I'll tell you what, you guys bring your beer and I'll bring my Bible."

Well, that went over like a lead balloon. At that, one of my friends tried to talk me out of being Born Again. He tried to tell me that he was Born Again once, but it's not a big deal. Jesus understands your need to get drunk and let off a little steam. Wow.

Until I started making friends at church, I went through a period of loneliness. I knew I was being tested. God was breaking me of the fear of man and wanting to make everyone happy. I was determined to pass my test and prove to God that I loved Him more than pleasing man and being the life of the party. I found this Bible verse:

> *So Jesus answered and said, "Assuredly, I say to you,
> there is no one who has left house or brothers or sisters or
> father or mother or wife or children or lands, for My sake
> and the gospel's, who shall not receive a hundredfold
> now in this time — houses and brothers and sisters and
> mothers and children and lands, with persecutions — and
> in the age to come, eternal life.*
> *— Mark 10:29-30*

The Holy Spirit encouraged me that, if I persevered, I would make friendships one hundred times deeper and richer than anything I have ever known. Everything Jesus promised is true. Whatever you give up for Jesus is seed. The harvest is always greater than the seed sown. If you have to give up toxic relationships, then Jesus will eventually reward you with a hundred-fold return. God has rewarded me with rich relationships based on a love for God and His Word. I have been accepted in the family of God (see Ephesians 1:6). I have many spiritual brothers and sisters; God is into a BIG family. Now I have family and friends all over the world. I persevered because I looked to the promised reward by faith.

Let's consider what Moses gave up and what his reward was:

- Moses gave up the temporary notoriety of being a prince of Egypt and became etched in the history of mankind for being a great lawgiver; the greatest of the Old Testament writing prophets.
- Moses gave up being a prince of Egypt and became so close to God Almighty that God Himself spoke to him face to face, as a man speaks to his friend (see Exodus 33:11).
- Moses gave up being a prince of Egypt to write and

compile, by the Holy Spirit, the first five books of the Bible. The Pentateuch (five books) is the foundation for the entire Bible. Everything subsequent was judged by it and had to agree with it (see Deuteronomy 12:32).

- Moses became a type of Jesus. Jesus was also tempted by the devil to give up His call and assume temporary rulership in this life. The devil offered him ruler-ship of all the kingdoms of the world (see Matthew 4:8-11). Jesus chose to look to an eternal reward rather than a temporary one, and we are to look at His example. Hebrews 12:2 – "Looking unto Jesus, the author and finisher of our faith, who for the joy that was set before Him endured the cross, despising the shame, and has sat down at the right hand of the throne of God." Instead, Jesus became the King of Kings and Lord of Lords for all eternity.

When we consider what we sacrifice for God and what He gives in return, it hardly measures up to be a sacrifice at all. I gave Him the brokenness of my life and became a joint heir with Christ!

> *The Spirit Himself bears witness with our spirit that we are children of God, and if children, then heirs — heirs of God and joint-heirs with Christ, if indeed we suffer with Him, that we may also be glorified together.*
> *— Romans 8:16-17*

Think about what a "joint-heir" is! If you are just an heir, then the inheritance would be divvied up and split among other heirs. If you are a "joint-heir" then all that Christ has is equally shared; we all share in the exceeding bounty of God's riches. If forgiveness of sins and a restored relationship with the true living God were all I received, that alone would be more than enough. But then He also decides to put the ring of sonship on my hand and elevate me to a position of nobility and kingship with Him for eternity.

> *"Do not fear, little flock, for it is your Father's good pleasure to give you the kingdom. Sell what you have and give alms; provide yourselves money bags which do not grow old, a treasure in the heavens that does not fail, where no thief approaches nor moth destroys. For where your treasure is, there your heart will be also."*
> *— Luke 12:32-34*

JOB RECEIVED DOUBLE FOR HIS TROUBLE

> *And the LORD restored Job's losses when he prayed for his friends.* ***Indeed the LORD gave Job twice as much as he had before.***
> *— Job 42:10*

> *My brethren, take the prophets, who spoke in the name of the Lord, as an example of suffering and patience. Indeed we count them blessed who endure.* ***You have heard of the perseverance of Job and seen the end intended by the Lord*** *— that the Lord is very compassionate and merciful.*
> *— James 5:10-11*

Many Christians focus completely on the suffering of Job and never consider his end. James instructs us to consider the relief of Job after he suffered. God's restoration, it seems, can often be double. It's not just getting back what you lost; the restoration is twice as much!

I was teaching from the pulpit about the suffering of Job and God's amazing restoration, and we were considering how long it was that Job had suffered. According to Job 7:3, it was months. According to Jewish tradition, it was a year. I was explaining that although Job's suffering was great, it wasn't an ongoing thing. Although grief may linger, it could have only been a year long. At this point in my sermon, a woman in the congregation yelled out, "NOOOOO!" I was taken off guard. I didn't quite know how to respond; so, I just repeated myself LOUDER and SLOWER so everyone could understand. Okay, I know, it was a little sarcastic and looking back it probably wasn't the wisest way to react, although I have to confess, I still laugh about it.

My point is that we tend to glorify suffering way too much. Although there can be much suffering in this life, I want to keep my eye on the victory on the other side. I am always going to preach about the victory on the other side. I am convinced that I can endure anything if I know it's temporary. This is the hope of the Christian. All suffering can work for me, not against me. To the world, suffering is just random injustice. To the Christian, "...all things work for good to those who love God, to those who are called according to His purpose." Romans 8:28b

> *For I consider that the sufferings of this present time are not worthy to be compared with the glory which shall be revealed in us.*
> *— Romans 8:18*

> *For our light affliction, which is but for a moment, is working for us a far more exceeding and eternal weight of glory, while we do not look at the things which are seen, but at the things which are not seen. For the things which are seen are temporary, but the things which are not seen are eternal.*
> *— 2 Corinthians 4:17-18*

> *For His anger is but for a moment,*
> *His favor is for life;*
> *Weeping may endure for a night,*
> *But joy comes in the morning.*
> *— Psalm 30:5*

Every one of these scriptures tell us to look to the victory on the other side of temporary suffering. I'm not trying to minimize the present pain that anyone may be going through. Nor am I suggesting that we pretend that it doesn't exist. What I am saying is that we endure by looking to the reward on the other side. David said in Psalm 23, "Yea, though I walk through the valley of the shadow of death." He confessed that he was walking through it, that this dark night of the soul was not going to last a lifetime. I have counseled with folks who have been through such great disappointment and despondency that they couldn't see an end. They felt so trapped that they couldn't comprehend that there could be any way of escape. They were tempted to commit suicide. Their sorrow was a hundred-pound bag of rocks on their neck and back weighing them down. The pain was so excruciating that they despaired of life.

At this point, the Holy Spirit must convince you that there is hope. But, YOU must cooperate with Him and begin to start BELIEVING that there is hope, which is belief that God has good things ahead. That God will get you through the valley of death. You must choose to look at the promise of victory.

> *I would have lost heart,* **unless I had believed**
> *That I would see the goodness of the LORD*
> *In the land of the living.*
> *— Psalm 27:13*

*Now may the God of hope fill you with all joy and peace
in believing, that you may abound in hope by
the power of the Holy Spirit.*
— *Romans 15:13*

We must make choose to begin to believe again. Once we make that move to believe, the power of the Holy Spirit comes rushing in to help us, and to open up a wellspring of hope in our hearts and minds. Then we must daily make this choice to believe and confess these scriptures. Eventually, the power of despondency *will* be broken. You may not even know when it left you. All you know is that you survived and things are looking up again.

Job survived the worst things anyone could ever go through, the death of his family, loss of all his livelihood and fortune, physical sickness and imminent death. Yet in the end, he was rewarded double for his trouble. How suddenly things can change from hopeless to hopeful. We must heed the exhortation of James and consider the end of Job. We need to look to the reward.

*Instead of your shame you shall have double honor,
And instead of confusion they shall rejoice in their portion.
Therefore in their land they shall possess double;
Everlasting joy shall be theirs.*
— *Isaiah 61:7*

YOUR WORK SHALL BE REWARDED

*For we are His workmanship, created in Christ Jesus for
good works, which God prepared beforehand that
we should walk in them.*
— *Ephesians 2:10*

Pathway to Promotion

We are not saved by our works; we are saved FOR good works. We cannot earn our salvation; it's a free gift to everyone willing to believe the good news and turn (repent) from what they know is wrong and begin doing works befitting righteousness. In the above verse, we are not only saved for a purpose and work, but we are a beautiful work: God's workmanship. The word for "workmanship" is the Greek word "poiema" from which we get the English word, "poem." God is making our lives into a stunning poetic expression to be read by others. The works we do for Him are a creative expression of our great love and appreciation for the freedom we have found in Christ. Our good works are an outward evidence of an immense inward change and a glorious declaration of what God is doing in our lives. We are not saved by our works, but the works expressed in prose and etched with love will be rewarded.

But you, be strong and do not let your hands be weak,
for your work shall be rewarded!
— 2 Chronicles 15:7

*Thus says the LORD: "Refrain your voice from weeping, and your eyes from tears; for **your work shall be rewarded**, says the LORD, and they shall come back from the land of the enemy. There is hope in your future, says the LORD, that your children shall come back to their own border.*
— Jeremiah 31:16-17

*For God is not unjust to forget **your work and labor of love** which you have shown toward His name, in that you have ministered to the saints, and do minister.*
— Hebrews 6:10

Look to the Reward

> *And whoever gives one of these little ones only a cup of cold water in the name of a disciple, assuredly, I say to you,*
> ***he shall by no means lose his reward.***
> *— Matthew 10:42*

Even the smallest good deed done in the name of Jesus will not be forgotten by God. We can't comprehend or imagine the vast expanse of grace-filled rewards that await the faithful believer. God is able to do exceedingly abundantly above all that we ask or think (see Ephesians 3:20). It has not entered the heart of man the things God has prepared for those who love Him (see 1 Corinthians 2:9).

My wife went through a season of great discouragement within our ministry. She had been betrayed, attacked and lied about by some folks that she loved and had deeply ministered to. The attacks were unrelenting and continued for a couple of years. It was also very difficult for me as a husband to protect and defend her. It was like an evil spirit that kept moving around from person to person to person. It almost caused us to quit ministry all together.

During that time I had a dream. In the first scene of the dream, I saw my wife in a casket. In the next scene, I saw her working in a flower garden, planting and tending to a vast array of colorful blooms. God's healing journey for her was found in flower gardens. When I shared the dream with her, she became very interested in horticulture. She has become very amazing with flower gardens. She astounds me with her memory of the names of all the diverse flora. God unlocked a hidden gifting in her and she is extremely creative with flower arrangements in pots and corner spots. When we visit nurseries together and walk among the vibrant lush green plants, the smell of fresh overturned dark soil and fragrant flowers reaching toward the sun give off an amazing energy. It's like you can feel the life-force of the plants absorbing right into your body. I totally get it why people are into farming and horticulture. God has put such powerful DNA energy into the seed to produce after its own kind. It's nothing short of miraculous to see the plants you've planted to grow and bloom. My wife was led to this scripture that has not ceased to encourage her:

> *Then I said, 'I have labored in vain, I have spent my strength*
> *for nothing and in vain; yet surely my just reward is*
> *with the LORD, and my work with my God.'*
> *— Isaiah 49:4*

What if you've worked hard and it seems fruitless? Does this mean that you have failed? The first thing that needs to be determined is, did you obey God to the best of your ability? I'm not asking if you made any mistakes along the way. I am asking if you generally obeyed God in the integrity of your heart. If the answer is YES, then quit beating yourself up. Our obedience is the determining factor as to whether or not we were successful, not whether people responded adequately.

How would you like to have the prophet Jeremiah's ministry? God told him right up front that he would NOT be successful in convincing people to heed his message. He told him that no one would listen, and they would harden their hearts, but then He told him to go and preach anyway (see Jeremiah 1:17-19). Jeremiah wasn't responsible for people's reactions; he WAS responsible for HIS action. God told the same thing to Isaiah (see Isaiah 6:8-13).

Listen to what the Lord told Ezekiel:

> "But the house of Israel will not listen to you, because they will not listen to Me; for all the house of Israel are impudent and hard-hearted. Behold, I have made your face strong against their faces, and your forehead strong against their foreheads. Like adamant stone, harder than flint, I have made your forehead; do not be afraid of them, nor be dismayed at their looks, though they are a rebellious house."
> — Ezekiel 3:7-9

Both the prophets and the apostles had to preach what God gave them whether the message was received or not. God could not judge a rebellious people until He gave them adequate warning. We must be obedient and be sincere to the message given us to share. If they dislike the vessel that the message came through, then that's on them.

My main point here is that we tend to think we are successful if our ministries and businesses grow overnight. We compare ourselves with others who confidently share the ten easy steps to their success. We always need to stay true to what God has called US to do. We are not rewarded by standards set by others, nor are we rewarded based on our own standards. The Lord of all the earth is the judge. He, and He alone, determines whether we are true to His call or not. We should always be praying for more fruitfulness, but we should also make sure we are true to ourselves and the call of God.

The great doctor and explorer David Livingston had two goals when he traveled inland from Cape Town, South Africa: to win souls and tribes to Jesus, and to map river routes into the heart of Africa to bring commerce that would end the slave trade. At the end of his life, with a sickened body from his herculean expeditions to map the Zambezi River and discover the source of the Nile, he felt like a failure. He hadn't discovered a useful river into Africa's dark interior nor had many converts. And yet, his work paved the way for many missionaries after him to win millions to Christ. His maps and writings of Africa brought colonization from Europe that civilized much of Africa and contributed to the end of the slave trade. We view our life and work one way, but God has a different perspective. We must be obedient to His call and trust the results and ultimate fruitfulness to Him. God is a rewarder of obedience.

> *And whatever you do, do it heartily, as to the Lord and not to men, knowing that from the Lord you will receive the reward of the inheritance; for you serve the Lord Christ.*
> *— Colossians 3:23-24*

Everything we do, we do as unto the Lord and not to men. God is the ultimate promoter and not people. When you have passed your test and it is time for your promotion, there is nothing man can do to stop it. Although the messages of the prophets and apostles were rejected by some, their words are still bearing fruit today and will continue to do so throughout eternity. Our obedience is the ultimate gauge of our reward, not the perceived results. Your work WILL be rewarded.

THREE FINAL THINGS

I was the chaplain for a Christian school and was overseeing my final service in that capacity. I received a new appointment to another church and community as a youth pastor and worship leader. As I was preparing for my final sermon of encouragement to the graduating class and other students, an impression from the Holy Spirit came to me that most of these students I would never see again in this lifetime. That in itself was sobering, but I also received a challenge from the Spirit, "If you knew this would be the last time you would see someone, what would you tell them?" I thought about it very hard and came up with these three basic things to say to these young students that I loved.

1. Put God first in everything.
2. Live peaceably with all men.
3. Don't allow your heart to become bitter.

I call this the **KISS** method of Christianity; **K**eep **I**t **S**imple **S**tupid. If you don't like the word "stupid" then replace it with "silly." If you don't like the word "silly" then I don't know what to do for you; you might have to make up your own acronym. This one works for me. Let's go over number one.

1. Put God first in everything

*But seek first the kingdom of God and His righteousness,
and all these things shall be added to you.
— Matthew 6:33*

If we keep God first in our life, everything seems to fall into place. Seek Him first in all your decisions. Consider His opinion before every major decision. Love Him with all your heart, mind and strength (see Matthew 22:37-40).

Put God first every day by reading your Bible (see Joshua 1:8). Put God first in your week by attending church every Sunday (see Hebrews 10:24-25). Put God first in your finances by giving tithes (10% of your income) and offerings to forward His work (see Malachi 3:8-12). Put God first in your relationships by following the Golden Rule:

"Therefore, whatever you want men to do to you, do also to them, for this is the Law and the Prophets" Matthew 7:12. (I told you this was simple.)

We also put God first when we acknowledge Him in all our ways and trust Him when we don't understand. He promises to not leave us directionless but to guide us and give us wisdom. Pray and consider God's opinion whenever you are making any major decisions. Don't recklessly tell God what you're going to do and demand that He bless it. Put Him first by acknowledging Him in those decisions and He promises to guide you with His wisdom (see James. 1:5).

> *Trust in the LORD with all your heart, and lean not on your own understanding; In all your ways acknowledge Him, and He shall direct your paths.*
> *— Proverbs 3:5-6*

It's as simple as that. He will never lead you wrong. If this was the only thing to remember, this would suffice.

2. As much as lies in you, strive to be at peace with all men

> *If it is possible, as much as depends on you, live peaceably with all men.*
> *— Romans 12:18*

When the Bible says, "If it is possible, as much as depends on you," it means there will be some situations where some people just don't want peace, or are incapable of giving you peace. You can desire restoration and reconciliation all you want, but the other party has to choose peace as well. You owe it to your conscience to do everything within your power to make peace; and if peace is an impossibility, then you must politely walk away from the relationship. You are not required to submit yourself to toxic and abusive people.

Divorce is a complicated thing. Not every situation is the same. It doesn't pay to paint with too wide of a brush and have overly simplistic answers without understanding the dynamics of each individual situation. I always challenge couples and ask them if they have done everything within their power to make this work. They owe it to their conscience to seek the Lord and do some deep soul searching. There are situations where a spouse has left and the person abandoned doesn't feel a release from the marriage. I will agree in prayer for them for as long as it takes until there is restoration, or they are fully convinced that God has released them. We must be honest and ask ourselves if we have done everything within our power to make peace before we move on.

3. Don't allow yourself to become bitter

> *Pursue peace with all people, and holiness, without which no one will see the Lord: looking carefully lest anyone fall short of the grace of God; lest any root of bitterness springing up cause trouble, and by this many become defiled.*
> *— Hebrews 12:14-15*

Opportunities seem to abound that would cause you to become bitter. Some injustices are worse than others, but God is faithful to always provide a way of escape (see 1 Corinthians 10:13). The Bible says that we must "look carefully," so we must pull weeds from the garden of our heart often; sometimes every day. Jesus said that in the last days the love of many would grow cold and that offenses would abound (see Matthew 24:10-13). In a lawless, loveless society that is brutal toward God and one another, offenses are sure to abound. The Bible warns us that a root of bitterness will not just affect us, but will infect many others. We do not sin in a vacuum; we are connected in relationship with others, and others can be poisoned by our bitterness. Bitterness can creep up on you and defile you slowly. You may not even perceive it is happening to you until you are overcome and spewing out raging vitriol.

If you are grieved by the bitterness of your soul, if you perceive a root of bitterness in your heart that has festered and become gangrenous, there is grace for you. If the above scripture states that you can fall short of the grace of God, then we have the power to choose His healing grace. You must take it. Jesus promises to heal the wounded soul. You CAN finish your race strong and maintain a sweet spirit. Out of your belly will flow a river of life. Grab hold of God's grace with all you have. Let His waves and billows wash over you.

YOU WILL BE TESTED BUT YOU CAN COME FORTH AS GOLD

0 But He knows the way that I take; when He has tested me,
I shall come forth as gold.
— Job 23:10

There are tests from God; there are demonic attacks and trials that come from being a member of the fallen human race. Whatever form the trial takes, God has promised that you shall come forth as gold. There is a place of maturity at which every Christian can arrive. I'm not saying that we ever arrive and don't need any further sanctification. I am saying that a believer in Christ can reach full bloom - a golden state of full adulthood. A place of becoming fathers and mothers, grandfathers and grandmothers in Christ. A place where a full life of experiences meets Bible knowledge. A place of peaceful wisdom and strength, settled in powerful grace.

> *Wisdom and knowledge will be the stability of your times, and the strength of salvation; the fear of the LORD is His treasure.*
> *— Isaiah 33:6*

> *Wisdom is with aged men, and with length of days, understanding.*
> *— Job 12:12*

Have you ever met one of these golden eagles: A stalwart Christian sage that brings intimidation into the camp of the enemy? Not all aged Christians are wise. Some have stunted their growth by refusing to change anymore and be moldable. Some have no understanding of the times and their advice is archaic. And yet, some have deep prophetic insight. Don't you want to get to that place? Don't you want to be the source of an artesian spring of wisdom?

I think that the chronological age of wisdom is different for everyone. A person may come to Christ early in life and have been blessed with wise mentors at a young age. This person may come into maturity relatively young, let's say in their thirties or forties. No matter how much Bible knowledge you have, or how young you come to Christ, you can't short change life experience.

I used to hate my birthdays. Every year just seemed to be a reminder that I had not achieved enough to feel good about myself. My fortieth birthday was the worst. I sat and "played happy" as I received the gag gifts of Rogaine and Depends Adult Diapers. All the cards had lame "over the hill" jokes. (I'm sure I deserved some of this because I'm a bit of a harasser.) Underneath the forced mirth I was a very unhappy person.

When I turned fifty everything changed. It's not that I had achieved this big "thing" that magically gave me personal self-worth. I crossed a mystical line in the spirit and I could sense it. For the first time, I felt like a spiritual father. This big Dad thing fell on me and it felt good. I didn't feel like I had to prove anything anymore and I accepted my new responsibility of being a mentor on a new level. After God brought me to this place of self-acceptance, certain outward achievements that I had always dreamed about started to happen. I was like an eagle that went through a mid-life molting process and began growing new feathers - golden feathers. He satisfies our mouth with good things so that our youth is renewed like the eagles. Psalm 103:5

Look to the reward of spiritual maturity and a place of being settled and at peace. Our heavenly Father is faithful to complete what He began in us (see Philippians 1:6). There is no promotion without a test, and when you are tested you shall come forth as gold.

www.ingramcontent.com/pod-product-compliance
Lightning Source LLC
Chambersburg PA
CBHW071232080526
44587CB00013BA/1575